The Silver Cradle

The Silver Cradle

Las Posadas, Los Pastores,
and Other Mexican American Traditions

Julia Nott Waugh

Foreword by Félix D. Almaráz, Jr.
Drawings by Bob Winn

University of Texas Press, Austin

Requests for permission to reproduce material from this work should be sent to Permissions, University of Texas Press, Box 7819, Austin, Texas 78713-7819.

LIBRARY OF CONGRESS CATALOGING-IN-PUBLICATION DATA

Waugh, Julia Nott, 1888–1958.
    The silver cradle/Julia Nott Waugh ;
  foreword by Félix D. Almaráz, Jr. ; drawings by Bob Winn.
        p.   cm.
    Collection of essays first published 1955.
    ISBN 0-292-77625-X (pbk.)
    1. Festivals—Texas—San Antonio. 2. Mexican Americans—Texas—
San Antonio—Social life and customs. 3. Mexican Americans—Texas—
San Antonio—Folklore. 4. San Antonio (Tex.)—Social life and
customs. 5. Folklore—Texas—San Antonio. I. Title.
GT4811.S25W38 1988
398.2'6'09764351—dc19   88-25133
                                                                    CIP

∞ The paper used in this publication meets the minimum requirements of
American National Standard for Information Sciences–Permanence of Paper
for Printed Library Materials, ANSI Z39.48-1984.

The church and some of the people in this book are composites. All names are fictitious except those of the family associated with the Chapel of the Miracles.

For

GERTRUDES ALONZO
superb Luzbel

and

FRANCISCO URIEGA
Parrado without peer

Contents

Foreword

In the first edition of *The Silver Cradle,* Julia Nott Waugh declared: "Everything recorded in this little book has occurred in San Antonio, and it may occur again tomorrow." Focusing mainly on customs and traditions that were "characteristic, significant, and apparently eternal" among Mexican Americans, the author, with graceful sensitivity, described a Hispanic cultural presence in San Antonio that neither time nor progress has erased.

Unencumbered by scholarly trappings and endowed with the perspective of a non-Catholic, Waugh immersed herself in the environment of West Side barrios, sometimes in freezing weather, to transcribe accurately performances of ethnic rituals or reenactments of churchyard theater. Replete with nuance and detail, she artfully recorded seasonal festivities, such as *Las Posadas, Los Pastores, Las Calaveras,* and liturgical observances of Holy Week.

In recent years these celebrations have attracted widespread support from neighborhoods beyond the boundaries of the West Side community. Following an American renaissance of interest in the Southwestern Borderlands during the 1960s, patriotic assemblies honoring Miguel Hidalgo's Grito de Dolores gradually assumed broader dimensions of public awareness. As reflected in the programs of an intimate band of dedicated participants, Waugh captured the essence of Mexican civic pride of an earlier period. Owing to a new consciousness, the customs, traditions, and values of Mexican American families depicted in *The Silver Cradle* are now appreciated by a much wider segment of the population.

Among significant changes in attitudes since 1955, when Waugh's book initially appeared, is popular acceptance of the term Mexican American, or even the emotionally charged Chicano, rather than the quaint cognomen of Mexican. Admittedly, the author preferred "Mexican" to acknowledge an indebtedness to persons who shared substantial bits of folklore. They were "of Mexican blood," she avowed, "and the manner of life which they perpetuate comes to them from Mexico and bears the imprint of that land."

Félix D. Almaráz, Jr.
13 June 1988
Feast Day of San Antonio de Padua

Acknowledgments

I wish to express appreciation to the College of Our Lady of the Lake for sympathetic and scholarly assistance in the library of that institution and for access to copies of two manuscripts: one of *Los Pastores* belonging to Don Leandro Granados, the other of the thesis on *Los Pastores* which was presented by the late Katherine Field Tarver for the Master of Arts degree at Southwestern University. Nor may I forget Mrs. Esther Vázquez, of the Biblioteca Mexicana; Mrs. Minnie Cameron, Reference Librarian at the San Antonio Public Library; and her assistant, Miss Elizabeth McCollister, all of whom have been ably and patiently helpful through the years.

I desire to acknowledge the contribution of Mr. Joel Quiñones Garza, who translated from the Spanish the greater number of the poems which I have used. I am also obliged to the American Folk-Lore Society for permission to use portions of their translation of *Los Pastores*, and to the Boston Music Company for permission to use part of their translation of the Mexican National Hymn.

Particular recognition is due two priests at the Church of Our Lady of Guadalupe: the Reverend Joseph B.

Carbajal, S.J., who has given me not only information but friendship; and the Reverend Carmen Tranchese, S.J., who is responsible for the preservation of many lovely customs and for the very existence of a band of *pastores* players whose enthusiasm grows and burgeons.

Most of all, I pay tribute to the many good Mexicans whose hospitality both material and spiritual I have enjoyed, and who have become my valued friends.

The Silver Cradle

CHAPTER ONE

The Bottom of the Pile

I am then seated in the lowest place,
I can no longer be deposed.
        —Luis Quintanilla

Polycarpo Méndez lives with his wife, Felicidad, their
five children, and an indeterminate number of relatives
in a three-roomed house in the Mexican quarter of San
Antonio. It is penetrated with the greatest ease by cold
in winter, heat in summer, and the gentle rain from
heaven regardless of season.

A few years ago it consisted of two small rooms worn

gray by time and weather. The Méndez family began to feel that their home was not only crowded but a little drear. So Polycarpo assembled some scraps of lumber, flattened some oil cans, and at the cost of considerable labor and a dollar-and-a-half in cash, added a third apartment. Then he painted the front blue, Felicidad arranged forty-five pots of begonias and ferns and jasmines before it, fastened bamboo cages inhabited by lovebirds and canaries on either side of the door, and began to hang her white and rose and blue and yellow washing on the line. The family felt, quite rightly, that they had a charming place to live in. A hydrant by the door and a toilet a few steps away are the only concessions to modernity, but the Méndez are a cheerful lot, and it is not their philosophy that happiness rises on a basis of plumbing.

Polycarpo's name, which means "many fishes," has no special relevance. Nor has that of his elder son, Plutarco, who is not historically inclined. But Felicidad is well-called: she is a happy, or at any rate a contented woman. Passing often through Alazán-Apache Courts, she looks wonderingly at the solid buildings of the San Antonio Housing Authority which shelter more than a thousand of the underprivileged Mexican families of San Antonio. She thinks tranquilly that it would be agreeable to live in a rainproof apartment with shades that pull up and down, a bath that functions, a gas stove and, miracle of miracles, an electric refrigerator. She knows that the Méndez qualify for occupancy: Polycarpo is a United States citizen whose income is sufficiently inadequate to meet the requirements of the Authority; they live in what is technically known as a substandard dwelling, and have neither communicable diseases nor a police record of consequence. They might, then, wear down the waiting list and eventually acquire such palatial quarters at a price which varies with economic conditions, is adjusted to the earnings of the family and to the number of minor children, and includes reasonable amounts of gas, electricity and water thrown in as one grand pilon.

To Felicidad and Polycarpo, however, the rental is always a large sum. And they are aware of the not immediately apparent benefits of their lot. In the first place, they are already a family of seven, including little grandmother. María del Refugio won't be an infant in arms next year, and in the nature of things other babies will come along. Even though they had a fine apartment with four bedrooms, in a short time they would be violating the strange rule that not more than two adults and an infant, or three children, may occupy one small chamber; and that boys and girls beyond the age of six must sleep in separate rooms. And what about the ramifications of the family? Nobody cares how many people inhabit that little house of theirs. Widowed aunts and orphaned cousins may stay as long as they like. Felicidad may take in any unprotected child who comes her way. They may put beds under the tree that spreads over their *casita* and sleep much of the year in the sweet night air. They may have dogs in the yard—the number, health and habits of those dogs being their own business. Pigeons may flutter over the roof, making a great mess. Sancho the goat, tethered all day in the coarse grass along the creek, still may call the place home. Felicidad may have a garden, a few rows of corn and gourds and tomatoes, among which delicate flowers flourish. And although she sees to it that the area in front of the house is clear, Polycarpo may litter all the rest of the place with an unbelievable assemblage of junk —parts of long-demolished automobiles, a broken-down cart, worn-out tubs, cans and bottles without number, all waiting to be put to heaven knows what good use. They may keep parked before the house the wreck of an automobile. It is the possession of the car that makes Plutarco spit on the fine new Courts. "Our automobile doesn't run," he says, "It has no tires if it did. But it is our automobile, and it can stand at our gate."

As for cooking facilities, Felicidad's little iron stove is a positive blessing. The beans, bubbling all day long and as far into the night as the heat lasts, come off with a soft, soupy quality that more modern methods are powerless to achieve. She is expert in the art of clapping the masa into thin, round tortillas which she cooks on its flat top. Her mother used to soak the corn in lime water, and spent hours of her life grinding it with a stone mano on a stone metate, but Felicidad buys the mash, admittedly inferior, at the Molino de Nixtamal down the way. The stove is, moreover, their only source of heat in winter. And when Felicidad runs out of fuel, she has only to give the boys a nickel (saved for such an imperative), and send them to the grocery for fifteen sticks of wood. Surely that is better than being obliged to have a lot of money on some set date, or being bothered, as are a few of her friends, by a young man who is always threatening to turn off the gas—and finally does. An electric refrigerator would be a marvelous toy, of course, but Felicidad doesn't have any greens and she thinks the proper thing to do with meat, if ever there should be a surplus, would be to dry it on a line in the yard.

Polycarpo and Felicidad have not only a floor, a roof of sorts, and a hydrant, they possess furniture. They have bought on the installment plan a shining, shoddily made bed and dresser. They put down pallets at night, of course, and an old iron bed stands in the yard. Most of their clothing they keep in trunks or boxes, the concept of closets not having penetrated more deeply than Alazán-Apache Courts. They own a backless bench, two rawhide-bottomed chairs, the wood smooth and shining from long use, and a metal chair painted blue, which oscillates at the will of the occupant. On the walls are enlarged photographs of the family (no Mexican is too poor to have his likeness made), pictures of La Virgen de San Juan de los Lagos who is much venerated hereabouts, Nuestra Señora de Guadalupe, and Franklin D. Roosevelt. On a shelf in the corner stands a figure of La Santísima, surrounded by paper flowers, a candle burning perilously before her. These three, the stove, the pictures, the altar, seem to the Méndez family the essential elements of a home.

It is quite possible that Polycarpo and Felicidad will pass all their days in this little house. They know that out of the money he earns keeping the yards of rich people on the other side of town they can pay about twelve dollars a month for rent. It is even thinkable that they will buy the place; members of their families, friends no better off than they, possess their own rooftrees.

Felicidad's sister, Otilia, lives in a tenement known

popularly, and even officially, as a corral (the word means a place where animals are kept) which her landlord calls a *colonia*. It consists of two long buildings, expanded cottages, with low-pitched roofs and long straight porches, facing each other across a narrow lane or court. Down the center is a parkway where red and green palma Christi and bananas and oleanders flourish nearly all the year. The family carries on in a front room, a small back room, and a section of the porch, and has access to a hydrant, toilets, and cold showers. For this accommodation they pay fourteen dollars per month, and for twenty dollars they could have four rooms. The place is hot most of the year, cold a little of the year, and crowded with people and things every day of the year. But on a fair soft morning when banana leaves are rustling, when there is the scent of flowers in the air, when birds are singing all down the long porches, and a green parrot takes the air in the drive; when men are sunning their brown torsos, and women sit on the steps nursing their babies and eternally combing their long, black hair—on such a day Otilia's home is a pleasant place to look upon.

Other corrales and shacks are cheaper, and exist quite without benefit of flowers and charm. Felicidad knows families who have no floors in their houses, no glass in their windows, who patch their walls with cardboard; she has friends farther out who buy water from an *aguador*, an old man who peddles that primal necessity at a ruinous price from a little donkey-drawn cart. He doesn't get rich, however. And to a family in great distress, he sometimes gives ten gallons or twenty.

On his way home from work Polycarpo passes the memorial to F. D. R. erected in the shadow of the city hall by the now defunct Comité Mexicano de Acción Cívica y Cultural. On the anniversary of the president's death, and on Mexico's Independence Day, he sometimes sees a group of his compatriots gathered there with flags and bands and banners to leave flowers, to pay tribute to "the good neighbor" and to all those "who like him died for freedom." Polycarpo likes to leave a flower, too.

At rare intervals Felicidad and her mother go over to view the metropolitan area around the city market. In that quarter they enter into an atmosphere truly Latin. First, there is the outdoor character of the life, the littleness of the enterprises. Men sit on the sidewalks beside small tables on which are displayed perfume, religious articles, and cheapest jewelry. Old fellows in vast hats arrange red tomatoes or silvery onions in careful pyramids. Women in black shawls set up shop with a low chair and a basket of tortillas covered with a clean cloth, or a bowl of finely cut *nopalitos*, the young leaves of the prickly pear, so cheap and, if you know how to treat them, so tasty. Beautiful fruit stands there are, presided over by Mary the Virgin, in which tomatoes and peppers, melons, oranges, bananas and pineapples and pomegranates are disposed to charm the eye. Felicidad and mama pause perhaps at a *baratillo*, a word which proclaims truly that a place is little and cheap. Seated at a table covered with bright-colored oilcloth, watched over by Our Lady of Guadalupe and a few Coca Cola girls, they treat themselves at a total cost of ten cents to *café con leche y pan*. Refreshed and inspirited, they go on their way.

They look longingly at arrays of cheap clothing. They

pass idly by multitudinous pawn shops filled with jewelry, with musical instruments, and elaborately wrought fire-arms. Nor are they attracted by bookstores displaying paper-backed editions (most of them from Barcelona) of *Aventuras de Pickwick, Ana Karenin, Los Tres Mosque-teros, Cuentos Orientales, Las Mil y Una Noches, Como Ganar Amigos e Influir Sobre las Personas, El Libro de los Remedios Mexicanos;* books on mental magic, the arts of love and bullfighting; and a pamphlet on the breeding, education, and preparation of cocks of combat. But they gaze desirously at religious medals, pictures, figures, of which there is no end. Sometimes they make a purchase.

They do not patronize the Farmacia Guadalupana with its two Virgins, its smiling photograph of F. D. R., and its staff of registered pharmacists. Nor do they enter the drugstore of the lovely name, the Botica del Socorro. They go instead to an *herbario* installed in the corner of a pottery and basket shop, and presided over by a young man who has, in his own eyes and those of his patrons, the attributes of a celestial chemist. He is surrounded by a marvelous array of herbs and seeds and charms: rattles from the dangerous snake, three of which hung around a baby's neck alleviate the miseries of teething; the forelegs of deer, which heated and rubbed on the affected member relieve neuralgia; roots of the pecan tree for pulmonary troubles, and of the century plant for ailments of the kidneys; beans to be heated and rubbed on the head for deafness; and the skin of the horned toad for ulcers, even cancer. A live horned toad strapped to the abdomen is said to be more effective, but the creatures are not usually stocked in San Antonio *herbarios*. Felicidad buys eucalyptus leaves for her mother's rheumatism. She could purchase them nearer home, but it is exciting to talk to the *herbolario*. She may acquire also a lump of *piedra imán*, the magnet which, in conjunction with one or three *colorines* (a particular kind of red bean), draws whatever is desired, even love, to its possessor. Or she may purchase a *milagro*, a small silver medal, which she has promised to the Lord of the Miracles on Ruiz Street. Then the ladies turn away from the world of buying and selling, back to the blue house under the great tree.

Now there is available to the Méndez, in addition to the celestial chemist, a wide variety of medical attentions. First, there are the saints to whom they pray, and whom they pay. Then, there are established in the quarter an immoderate number of doctors, a few of whom have claims to distinction. One of these men, after having contributed much to Latin-American well-being here, departed to enter the public health service of Mexico, and eventually to become chief of the departmental health officers for the whole country. Another left his office on Buena Vista Street (which has no view at all) to serve as ambassador from Mexico to a half-dozen countries, as delegate to the United Nations and various international labor conventions, and finally as Director General of Tourism in his own land. A third, exiled by the Revolution, has taken root in San Antonio. Personally picturesque and professionally able, he is patriarch of perhaps the largest medical family in the town: three of his sons and a son-in-law are doctors of medicine, a fourth son is a dentist, a grandson is a medical student, and a daughter is a pharmacist. They have established themselves in adjacent buildings, connected by a green garden. The drugstore is, of course, the province of the daughter. Its dark woodwork, tiled floor, crystal chandeliers and beautiful old apothecary jars speak of an elder day. Through a doorway is the waiting room of "the doctor senior." High and bare, supported by granite columns and dominated by a great "Descent from the Cross," it has the character of a temple. But the offices of the sons, across the patio and facing on another street, are as modern as tomorrow.

Medical fees are of necessity scaled to the income of the patient, but any fee at all is often beyond Polycarpo's capacity to pay. An inadequately financed Health Department supplies such help as it can, as do various religious and philanthropic organizations. Happily there is in this field no quarrel between Church and State. The settlement houses, established by many denominations for the benefit of the Mexican people, and apparently quite unsectarian in their labors, co-operate with officials in conducting surveys, in disseminating information, and in supplying plants for free clinics which are staffed, or partially staffed, by Health Department personnel. But in a community in which too many families live in too few houses, those houses infected and reinfected with disease, in which thousands of people are improperly nourished and tuberculosis is rife—in such a community all the efforts which have yet been made are but little drops of water on parched sands of human need.

It is well for their tranquility of spirit, perhaps, that women like Felicidad Méndez and her mother prefer, in the usual run of things, to get along with herbs and miracles. For the birth of a child, however, ordinary as is that event, they do make special arrangements. All of little grandmother's fifteen children were delivered by midwives. These women were licensed in San Antonio in 1809 (the fees were spent that year on repairs to the church and work in the cemetery), and they were not very long ago the obstetricians of the quarter. In the early thirties, however, the medical department of the Relief sent budding doctors among poor people. The young men must have acquitted themselves well, for women who were at first shy or afraid now take pride in being cared for by a *médico* rather than by a *partera*. The midwives still do a thriving business, however, delivering a large proportion of the Latin-American babies of the town, and being highly thought of by their own people. They vary in years from youth to great age; in education from illiteracy to incomplete college training. The Health Department, recognizing that they fill a need, instructs and supervises them as well as it is able. Las Damas Profesionales, which holds a state charter, has long been a respected organization. About the many *parteras* of whom the authorities have never heard, they naturally can do nothing. That midwives are valued by their patients is understandable. What doctor will deliver a baby for seven dollars? Or for thirty dollars will give ninety days of prenatal and forty of postnatal care, and preside over the delivery with competence? Above all, what doctor comes in to bathe and do the necessary for mother and child on the three days following the birth?

The baby's chances, however, are slim. There have been

years when three times as many Latin-American as Anglo-American infants have died in San Antonio. That was due largely to premature births, to debility, and diarrhea among the well-loved *niñitos* of the west side.

Having been successfully born and properly bathed, those of the Méndez children who survive are in due course exposed to education. Juan Bautista and Agapita go to a public school near Alazán-Apache Courts where the training is slanted to meet the particular needs of little Latin-Americans. That policy is very necessary, for during the winter months when families are in from seasonal labor treks, more than half of the children in the public schools of the towns are of Mexican origin. And the number is increasing. Little grandmother, who was born here, speaks English not at all; but her daughter manages the language with some facility, and her grandchildren are from an early age bilingual. At school they learn to read and write and figure, to brush their teeth and to salute the flag. If they were enrolled in one of the many institutions maintained by the Catholic Church (and they would be if their parents were able to pay a small tuition) they would learn manners and prayers.

Plutarco goes to the great high school not far from home which has an enrollment almost exclusively Mexican. There he comes under the guidance of an administration which begins at the ground in its effort to make of him a good citizen and a happy human being. He may take a hot shower if that seems desirable, and he would surely be sent home if he needed delousing. He has a physical check up every six weeks, and should it be revealed that he was underfed, some sort of job by which he might earn lunch money would be found for him. The free soup kitchen established during a time of severe economic depression was an outstanding failure. Hungry children wouldn't go near it.

In addition to his academic work, Plutarco has access to training in all sorts of arts and crafts and trades. He might have instruction in cabinetmaking and furniture upholstering, in auto painting or body and fender work. He might learn to be a draughtsman or a printer. But he has chosen auto-mechanics, and he expects to be graduated at the end of three years as an advanced apprentice. If he is any good, he can always get a job—nobody cares how dark-skinned is the fellow who crawls under his car. And there is something about wheels going round that is exciting to Plutarco Méndez.

When Agapita and Refugio come along they may have prenursing courses if they show sufficient aptitude in that direction. Or they may learn dressmaking, an art in which Mexican girls are often talented. And whether they like it or not, they will take thorough grammar school courses in domestic science. Nobody knows, perhaps, what such training means to the future families of these children, but it is sadly true that they resist domestic service with all their strength and will.

Boys and girls alike may have instruction in typewriting and shorthand, if they make "B" in English. They may hammer out metal jewelry and trinkets; they may work with plastics; they may learn photography and commercial engraving. They may do wood carving, a field in which these people are especially gifted; or they may take up leather work, which will lead to profitable employment in saddle shops of the region. Those students who show interest and ability will be making posters and illustrations for the school annual. But the objective of the art training in this school is severely practical: a livelihood. Plutarco plays in the band. Juan Bautista will surely belong to the orchestra—one day he may have a group of his own musicians and make good money playing for dances. When the time comes little Agapita, who sings like a bird, will be a member of the choral club. At Christmas there is special music, and a tree in every room. School is for many children a release, a place of pleasure.

The principal takes justifiable pride in the fact that no graduate has ever been convicted of a serious offense. He is persuaded that for these people "education pays." Although it is true that more Latin-Americans go to college from his school than from any institution in the San Antonio area, he knows that children like the Méndez are more likely, for every reason in the world, to come out skillful workmen and cheerful citizens than scholars of any variety. It is sometimes easier, however, for ambitious young Mexicans to get training than to get jobs. A degree of resistance to them exists in certain types of employment due, in some instances, to prejudice whole and unadulterated, in others to unhappy experience. The principal believes that the difficulty springs chiefly from a feeling against color, that a pale-skinned youth is acceptable where a darker friend would not be tolerated. "It is," he says, "purely a matter of pigmentation." He should know. He spends the years of his life dealing with the problems of Latin-Americans in San Antonio. Certainly he has every reason to believe that children like Plutarco,

The Bottom of the Pile

Agapita, Juan Bautista, eventually Concepción and little Refugio, will have better jobs, better homes, better food, better health, and that they will give their children a better chance than Felicidad and Polycarpo with all their love and labor have been able to accomplish.

After school, and at any hour on Saturday, the Méndez children may stop at the Administration Building of Alazán-Apache Courts, or at the Community House near their home which happens to be operated by a Protestant church. At either place they will be submitted to a program of classes and pleasures calculated to make of them good citizens of the neighborhood, of San Antonio, of the world. Polycarpo and Felicidad go sometimes to see an educational film, or to sit in on a discussion of current affairs. They have on these occasions a sense of entering into a larger world, of satisfaction in mere space and order.

The quarter itself supplies amusement of a less purposeful sort. There exist west of the city hall cinemas of varying degrees of comfort which supply entertainment of varying degrees of timeliness. The grandest of these is in the Casa de México, an edifice of steel and tile and glass in which are situated a small auditorium used for cultural events, a library sponsored by the Mexican government, the consulates of Mexico and other Latin-American countries, as well as the offices of business and professional men and of many organizations. In the theater superior Spanish and Mexican films, together with a few from Hollywood, are shown, and a good deal of emphasis is laid on music and vaudeville.

The smaller houses go on their somewhat erratic ways.

Prices rise and fall with the state of the nation, and in bad years their managements are likely to institute certain agreeable customs. A poor little movie may admit women for two cents on Tuesday and Thursday of every week. "It is necessary," says the director, "to do something for the ladies." And the better theaters may welcome two patrons for the price of one on Thursday and Friday. On those days a boy has only to wait near the entrance for some amiable and unaccompanied individual to come along, and to ask, with an upturned face and the flicker of an eyelash, to go in with him. Since benefactor and beneficiary part at the door it costs no more than a nod to make sure that the child, at least, will pass a fine evening. Thus it is that lads like Plutarch and John the Baptist Méndez have viewed at a smelly little theatre westerns of the earliest and purest variety (contemporary productions for all that), British costume pieces, and an occasional "A" picture that was popular throughout the country two or three years earlier. At the better houses they have seen Mexican and Hollywood films, British and American documentaries, newsreels, and such a diverse array of stars as Jorge Negrete and Noel Coward, Cantinflas and Charles Chaplin, María Félix and Ingrid Bergman. It is interesting to observe that here as in Spain it is first the religious, then the horror pictures, that draw the largest crowds, inspire the warmest enthusiasm.

The women of the family do not, of course, avail themselves of this friendly opportunity. But once in the spring, and again in winter, Felicidad and her mother make an expedition to the cinema. On a day of Holy

The Bottom of the Pile

Week they walk up to a shabby little playhouse in their neighborhood to see the life of Christ presented on a flickering screen by actors gotten up in such yards of billowing cambric, such lengths of rope hair, in a setting of such myriads of cotton flowers, as one did not know existed. The place is full of women smiling happily through the scenes of the nativity, weeping inconsolably at what appears to be the news of the crucifixion. And in the month of December the ladies of the Méndez household betake themselves, at a considerably greater outlay of money and energy, to a well-established small theater over near the city market. There they see elegantly if academically presented the story of the Virgin of Guadalupe: how she appeared to the Indian, Juan Diego, four hundred years ago; how the roses which he picked at her bidding were transmuted into a picture of her holy self; how she became the patroness of the Mexican people. *"Non fecit taliter omni nationi,"* ("He has not dealt so with any nation") is her legend.

But the theatrical event of the year so far as the Méndez family is concerned falls on December 23. Toward eleven in the evening they proceed in a body, washed, combed, shone, and in a state of high excitement to a small, crude cinema, there to participate in the Mexican version of bank night. Even an occasion so commercial has an element of poetry, for it is not hard cash, it is not even government bonds that are at stake. It is fifteen little white goats which are to be delivered at midnight to the holders of fifteen lucky numbers; it is Christmas dinner, juicy and luscious, for fifteen happy families. Years ago when Polycarpo and Felicidad first were married they won a kid, and they have been going back unsuccessfully ever since. But they are not unhappy, "*Así es la vida.*"

Juan Bautista, with Concepción by the hand, lingers to gaze at the appealing little creatures which have been milling and bleating all the week in a pen set up before the theater. He chooses among them. "Let's have that one. And let's not kill him, *mamacita,*" he begs. "Let's keep him to play with Sancho."

Polycarpo has bought tickets, and the family enters with processional dignity. The house is not crowded, for the price has been raised to a fantastic level. They sit quietly through a short comedy, through a travelogue in which they watch the great world ski (they don't know why) at Chamonix, play golf at Cannes, and swim at Acapulco. It is something to see, but the audience is only waiting. Not until midnight do people sit on the edge of their chairs. Then, as the numbers are called, as the fortunate go forward to claim their Christmas feasts, there is not only thunderous applause, there is general happiness. Felicidad is rigid and smiling, the children are wide awake and eager. It is fine that someone is getting something for little. And as the family troops out in the chill morning of Christmas Eve, with no *cabrito,* only dark-faced Refugio asleep in her father's arms, they feel rewarded. They have indulged their passion for the lottery, they have participated in an occasion.

Such pleasures are fine and unfailing, but the focus of life for the Méndez family is the church of Jesús y María. The old grandmother goes there every day to pray, and they all go often. For these Latin-Americans whose lives are hard, who feel not seldom that every man's hand is against them, find in the climate of religion food for their essential needs: beauty and drama and a sense of refuge. Now it must be understood that much of the activity of a Mexican parish arises at the initiative of the people themselves. The priests know more or less what is going on. They may aid, or at any rate abet, an undertaking. But it is men like Polycarpo, women like Felicidad who, against a backdrop of factories and X-rays and automobiles and airplanes, imbue with life their Spanish and their Indian past. It is they who are forever bringing fruits from their fields, flowers from their gardens, offering those little plays and songs and dances that delight their inmost soul.

On the name day of the good pastor, Father Nepo, Felicidad and Agapita rise before dawn to join women and children in singing *mañanitas* beneath his window. On the feast of Our Lady of Guadalupe, old Damaso appears from nowhere with twenty gayly dizened children, the little matachinas, to present in terms of dance the story of Malinche and Cortés, the struggle of Spanish against Indian power. And on the following Sunday evening Jesús with his Chichimecas—men in vast feather headdresses, rattling gourds, clicking bows and arrows—offers to the gentle Virgin of the Christians the wild dances of a primitive people. On the nine nights before Christmas, children move in procession down the aisle to sing at the church door the plea of Mary and Joseph for shelter in the little town of Bethlehem. Sometime during the weeks that follow, perhaps many times, Doroteo Domínguez presents a nativity play conceived in a Benedictine monastery during the middle ages. In mid-January people bring their animals, from canaries to cats, to be blessed and sprinkled. And on Good Friday night they watch with deep emotion eleven old apostles carrying their dead Master to his entombment.

These are the offerings, eternally repeated, of people like the Méndez who, accepting fate, living with a sense of continuity, out of poverty and piety create the poetry of the poor.

CHAPTER TWO

The Silver Cradle

High among the pleasures of the Méndez children are the Christmas ceremonies sponsored by Agapita's godmother and everybody's friend, that woman of character, Graciana Reyes. Graciana is patroness in her neighborhood of *Las Posadas*, the search of Mary and Joseph for shelter in crowded Bethlehem. And in her home are enacted, faithfully every year, *la acostada* the laying down, and *la levantada* the taking up, of the infant Jesus.

Now Graciana hasn't a soft bed, nor a pair of silk stockings, nor a hat of any description, but she does possess a little silver cradle in which they lay the newborn Child in the second hour of Christmas morning, there to rest until the night of Candlemas. Delicately made, severely plain, this little six-inch crib is the chiefest of her treasures and the pleasure of her heart. It is a treasure, not because it is of *plata pura*, not for the sake of the Mexican gold pieces on the corners, but because around it cluster rituals intimate and charming which seem to this broad-hipped, childless woman to be peculiarly her own. It is a symbol of pleasure because these ceremonies are the reason, or the occasion, for a series of little parties, culminating in two great ones at which she is glowing hostess to her world.

But first of all, what is *Las Posadas*? And how does it concern the silver cradle? That is what you are going to hear.

It is a novena made in Mexican homes and churches on the nine nights preceding Christmas day. The words mean simply "the shelters" or, derivatively, "the inns"; and the content is the search of Joseph and heavy-bodied Mary for hospitality before her time shall come. In the churches it is practised with varying degrees of elaboration and of charm, with a simplicity tending toward the bleak. But in small houses on bright thoroughfares or down dim alleyways, it takes on warmth and color, a gentle Mexican merriment, the gaiety of Christmas as a feast of homes.

The faded red house of Graciana and Juan Angel stands on a busy street in a poor, but by no means the poorest, section of San Antonio. Automobiles and motorcycles, frail hand-pushed carts, and great lumbering buses pass eternally before it. It is a ramshackle abode without much comfort, but for the quarter spacious. One room is for sleeping, one is for cooking, and one, believe it or not, is specifically for eating. Another is a little store where they sell wood, paper sacks of charcoal, handfuls of groceries, and wonder-working remedies known to Graciana and her kind. The remaining apartment is given over much of the year to the vastest and most elaborate *Nacimiento* hereabouts. Now this is saying much, for a crib or a crèche or a place of the Birth is part of the Christmas scene in very many homes of Mexican San Antonio.

In the house of Graciana it takes up a good half of an eight-by-ten room, and reaches to a vaulted roof. Into its making have gone an incredible aggregation of humble, unrelated treasures: a railroad yard, a military encampment; a swimming pool on the banks of which repose, in company with Kewpie dolls, most improper bathing beauties; a small, red-curtained hotel which looks distinctly rakish; uncounted tiny dishes; a gladiator; a Mexican dancing girl; Adam and Eve under a palm tree; a Harlem band; Jesus Christ being flagellated by a Roman soldier; pictures of the Last Supper, of a stag at bay, and of Annette, Cecile, Yvonne, Marie, and Emilie Dionne—these and a thousand things besides. It is garishly lighted, it is flowered and embowered—a glorified Mexican toy shop, the Christmas stockings of children who have no other. And in the center, high up, it becomes a shrine. Here are a gilded St. Anthony and a Greek goddess finely formed in clay; here are the manger, the ox, the ass, the shepherds, and a foretelling crucifix. Here are Mary, Joseph and the Child. Only the figure of the baby Jesus is essential, but for Graciana elaboration is a custom and a pleasure.

During the second week in December there is a great stir in this usually placid household. The room of the *Nacimiento* is being scrubbed with pious thoroughness, the curtains washed, the hundreds of objects wiped and sorted; and the shelf, which is the base of the whole vast creation, contrived by supporting wide boards on two old dressers. Graciana and Juan Ángel work early and late. Even so, this aging pair could never accomplish the task without the aid of Paz and Fortunato, teenaged lads of the neighborhood, who come on four evenings to make an offering of climbing and nailing and high reaching. Then, on the fourteenth or fifteenth of the month, Graciana turns to a task which can no longer be delayed: the preparation of the *andas*. This little hand-borne float on which the holy pilgrims travel on the nine nights of their wandering is simply a shallow box, inverted, with openings in the sides through which poles may be passed, and on the flat surface arches forming the framework for a shelter. But naturally Graciana wishes her *posada*, as the children call it, to be both beautiful and various. She tears off the rich red and green of last year's decoration; she covers the floor with plaited white paper; she entwines the arches with paper vines on which pink roses blossom; and she sprinkles the whole with silver, making a gleaming, flowery float on which the blessed pair shall travel. Then she sets old Joseph and young Mary in their places. Their way was cold and bleak and sad in Bethlehem of

Judea. In Bethlehem of San Antonio it shall be delicate and shining.

On the last day of all, December the sixteenth, the room is by no means ready. But Fortunato has renewed the tinsel letters on the wall:

V. J. M. y J.
(Viva Jesús María y José)
19——

And Paz has made an arch of cedar boughs to frame the crib. Graciana covers the bare shelf on which it is to be assembled with a lace-edged cloth, sets thereon the *andas,* and disposes about it plants and candles.

Then comes an almost sacramental moment. She climbs onto a sturdy chair, unlocks a high-hung cabinet, takes out that small cradle of pure silver, and regards it with affection. Getting painfully down, she addresses herself to rubbing and shining its elegant plain bars, the gold pieces on the corners, the three *milagros* it has attracted. Her eyes fall on the figures of Mary and Joseph, waiting on their little float, and she begins to tell the tale of the families who will receive them when they go pleading. The Holy pair will be borne from this house down busy streets and through quiet ways to the home of Felicidad Méndez, there to repose the night; from the *casa* of Felicidad they will be taken to that of Saturnina; from the small house of Saturnina to the *colonia* where ancient Cruz carries on her life; and so every night, until on Christmas Eve they come back to her own door. She reflects with satisfaction that Magdalena Montemayor, who

The Silver Cradle

has lead the singing faithfully for seventeen years, will come again this Christmas season. She thinks affectionately of Felicidad's aunt, Constanza, the good woman who gave the silver cradle to the little Jesus, who long ago was *madrina* of *la acostada*, who passed on to her niece that privilege and duty. Rubbing and remembering, Graciana forgets her tired bones. She is happy. And when at last the gracious task is finished, she climbs again onto a chair, opens the cabinet, and locks in the cradle, radiant for its radiant visitant.

Being in a mood for pleasant doing, she goes to her great wardrobe, takes out a pottery jar, and onto the table pours a pile of copper and silver, pennies and nickels and dimes, a rare quarter. This is money saved by every sort of sacrifice of comfort, of well-being, and of pleasure, for her great feasts of Christmas Day and Candlemas. She makes the coins into little stacks, she counts slowly, she smiles contentedly: this year again there will be enough.

That night the house is bright with the raw glare of unmitigated electricity. And whatever the weather may be, the door stands open. Why not? There is nothing to be kept out, there is nothing to be kept in. No burden of physical comfort hangs about the necks of these people. Young girls come, and small children; mothers with new babies, who cannot readily go far from home; old women who find in such occasions companionship, life, and color. The hostess is beaming, everyone is quietly gay. Then, about eight-thirty, there is an influx into the house of Graciana, people coming from *Las Posadas* in the church of Jesús y María. Among them is Magdalena the faithful, a small, brown vibrant woman endowed with a beautiful quietude. A familiar of the house, she sits near the *andas*, waiting.

Into this tranquil company comes Graciana, shoulders and graying head wrapped round with black *rebozo*. Lighting the candles before the Pilgrims, she kneels and begins the service of the evening. The scent of cedar boughs, candles burning straight and true, that good woman praying. Behind her, kneeling women, kneeling children. The Rosary, voices raised in song, the invocations and petitions of the litany. This is the service of the Church, all the people know it well.

"*Ave María purísima,*" they murmur, coming to their feet. Candles are distributed. Juan Ángel comes to lift out the *andas*, and Agapita sets on the heads of Mary and Joseph their little straw hats. Then through the door the procession passes: four girls, each with taper in hand, bearing the *andas*; two by two, with wavering lights, the children; after them the women; at the very end Graciana, walking heavily, shading with her hand a candle.

Down the brightly lighted, busy street they move, pausing at an intersection for a lull in the hurrying traffic. Mary and Joseph wait patiently while the Fords and motorcycles and the Kelly Field buses go purposefully by. The Mexicans have the years of their lives, the Pilgrims have eternity, in which to cross that street, to find that manger. There is at last a space between onrushing cars, a momentary clearance, and the procession crosses over. It turns into a maze of small homes with Christmas trees or Christmas stars shining in their windows. And taking an uneven road these forty marchers, or fifty, come at last to the little house under the great tree where the Méndez live. Within the circle of Felicidad's plants they halt. Before the door the silvery *andas*, behind it women and children massed, light of candles falling on dark faces. The door opens and figures slip inside. Then begins the singing. The voice of Magdalena, resonant and sure, implores "shelter to rest" for

> Poor pilgrims who, disconsolate,
> Seek shelter on a foreign soil.

From within comes the refusal,

> We have no room, it is too late at night,
> There is no lodging anywhere.

The children join in the second plea,

> Take pity on us, we ask for shelter,
> We call heaven to witness our pain.

Again the denial,

> Not a single place is vacant here,
> People without number occupy it all.

Candles wavering, people singing in the night. They are ages and ages removed from neon signs and express trains, from airplanes and swift cars, these Mexicans gathered before a door in Bethlehem. This is not true. They are not removed. They are of a pastoral simplicity, but they are of the continuity of life.

Once more the appeal,

> Open your doors unto us two unfortu-
> nates
> Who wearied with travel beg rest.

The Silver Cradle

Once more the demand,

> Who knocks at this unseemly hour, in
> frozen night
> At the inn to beg shelter?

Then the revelation,

> Poor spouses address you, Mary and Joseph,
> Whom God has sent to implore your mercy.

The door opens, soft light falls into the darkness. There is welcome to "spouses innocent and chaste." They enter, Mary and Joseph and all the company, into a small room gently lit by oil lamps, rigorously scrubbed, and for this one night quite bare. The bed has been taken down—for any function in these little houses beds are taken down— the dresser has been pushed into a corner, and the three chairs set in a row. The altar, a bower of oleander branches dark and severe blossoming with great red waxen roses, is adorned with pictures of Our Lady of Guadalupe and a dancing girl nude to the waist. Candles in milk bottles burn before it.

The center of the room is full, quite full, of candle-carrying children. Against the walls dark-clad women stand, and through the doorway vague forms recede into the shadows of the kitchen. The hats are removed from the heads of the Pilgrims, the *andas* is set in the waiting bower. The people stand to sing their joy. They kneel to repeat an Act of Contrition, the Prayer for All the Days. Freely they sing,

> Fond travelers, humble pilgrims,
> Jesus, Mary, and Joseph,

With lodging do I give thee
My heart and soul as well.
Most beautiful of pilgrims,
Compassionate María,
I offer thee my spirit
To be this night my lodging.

There follows the reading of the First Journey of Mary
and Joseph in Bethlehem, the prayer to St. Joseph, the
nine-times repeated *jaculatoria,*

Jesus, Joseph, and Mary,
I offer to you for dwelling place
My heart and my soul.

Ritual gives over to merriment, to conversation, food,
and games, occasionally to dancing. Felicidad might serve
spiced chocolate and small, rich cakes; or she might offer,
as most of the hostesses do, only fruit with little bags of
nuts and cheapest candy. But she has chosen to provide
that characteristic delight of Mexican children's gatherings, a *piñata.* She invites her guests into the yard where
a lamb with red and green paper wool, dangling from a
wire stretched across an open space, disconsolately awaits
his fate. And his fate is to be pulled up and down, this way
and that while blindfolded children, turned around and
around to confuse their sense of direction, and given the
most contradictory advice by shrieking spectators, try to
hit him with a stick. For concealed within his colorful
exterior is a pottery jar filled with sweets. The first con-
testants haven't a chance. But when a good proportion of
the youngsters have done their hopeless best, the gods of

this particular machine, a man named Polycarpo and a boy called Plutarco, begin to relent, to jerk the *piñata* less suddenly, to leave it now and then within reach. So, eventually, the belly of the red and green lamb is broken, candy flies in all directions and the children scramble for it. Nobody gets much, but everybody has a fine time. To the women sitting on the wash bench or where they can, Felicidad passes dishes of sweets. Among them there is pleasant talk, the telling of tales. But Graciana's is the dominating presence, and when she rises the evening is finished. With many phrases and many embraces, she says goodnight. The gathering troops into the street and scatters through the darkness.

Tomorrow night a coming back—prayers and songs, at the very last voices raised in pretty thanks:

> Greatly indebted,
> We'll go on our way,
> Reward for your deed,
> From heaven we pray.

> Our gentle Lord protect thee
> And give thee peace divine,
> If you this night receiv'd us,
> Eternal joy is thine.

> Fare thee well, oh, workers,
> We leave thy humble inn,
> In payment holy Mary
> Will cleanse thy hearts of sin.

Points of light wavering down a misty street, turning into an open space where little houses, above their doors

Christmas lanterns burning dimly, stand amidst their gardens. People crowding onto a narrow porch, the pleas, the refusals, the revelation. So every night straight up to Christmas Eve. Then—ah, then—the weary pilgrims come back to Graciana's house. Tonight it is ready and waiting. There are the entreaties, the denials, the joyful admittance; people pressing into that bright, welcoming room, before that marvelous *Nacimiento* setting their burden down. The happy songs, the reading of the Ninth Journey, the sense of Christmas on the threshold.

Las Posadas has now come to its end. But the children are eager to gaze on the glories of that ever wonderful crib. They slip back into the little room, they fill it. There is pressure, perhaps, but there is no struggle—when a place is full, it is full. The older boys who are here tonight, the many teenaged girls, observe and pass on. But the little children stand dreaming, possessing these beauties every one: the railroad tracks, the soldiers, the great pig, the polar bear clambering on the rocks, the pink nosed lamb with violets on his chest, the multitudinous small dishes and decorations. Agapita is eager to aid her god-mother, to answer instantly any call for service. The women sit about a room with open doors and cold stove, talking a little together. Nothing happens. But that is of no moment—quietude is the perfect achievement of the Mexican people.

It may be that Christmas Eve is a mild night of almost summer warmth; or it may be that the wind blows shrewdly and a cold rain beats down on this and thousands of huddled poor homes. But without regard to weather, toward eleven o'clock the company slips away to the Mass of the Cock—the cock that announced, they say, the birth of Christ.

Graciana does not go with them. She is occupied to capacity with affairs personal and domestic. For her this is a function of many facets: the night of the Birth, the holy night, the night when the Pilgrims come home again. It is also an occasion for expansive hospitality. Wonderful things are happening in the brightly lighted, succulently steaming kitchen of the red house: chickens are simmering, rich mole is preparing, pots of beans and pots of rice are bubbling, piles of tortillas are heating, gallons of coffee are boiling; and, rarest treat of all, great pans of pudding stand ready and waiting.

But let it be well understood that magnificent as is this food, rich and rare as are these odors, the feast is a by-product, an event wholly subsidiary to a religious act with which the Reyes bring in Christmas morning. Juan Ángel lifts the figures of Mary and Joseph from the *andas,* and places them on an upper level of the *Nacimiento.* Then Graciana interrupts her humming busyness to make the final preparations: breathing heavily, hair curling damply about flushed face, she mounts a third time on a solid chair, unlocks the little cabinet, and takes therefrom the figure of the Baby Jesus and his shining silver cradle. She handles them with love and pride, caressingly she sets them in some small vacant space amidst the toys and treasures. Then she returns a little solemnly, with an air of removal, to her labors in the kitchen.

Slowly, under the stars, or hurriedly, whipped by a bitter wind; warm and tranquil, or blue-faced, wet, and cold, the people come back again. However bleak the night, they come in to shelter, but not to comfortable warmth. For, although wood is piled high, although the host is a merchant of fuel and the hostess the spirit of hospitality, it does not remotely occur to anyone that a fire might be lighted. The grownups sit huddled in coats and shawls, the babies are well wrapped and sleeping. There is a good deal of movement, of quiet gaiety, among the boys and girls. Everybody is happy to participate in a well-loved rite, to be present at a grand party.

In the little room the *Nacimiento* gleams. Polycarpo and Felicidad arrive a little breathless, with the air of coming on some special mission. As indeed they do. They are *padrino* and *madrina* of *la acostada*, the laying of the Child in the manger. Greeting the assemblage, embracing Graciana, they go immediately about the ceremony of this early morning. Holding lighted candles, they kneel on either side of a chair on which repose the cross-faced Spanish Christ and his little bed. The room is full of song as Felicidad wets cotton in jasmine-scented perfume and bathes most thoroughly that small waxen figure. She lays the well-washed Baby on a silvered dish which she and Polycarpo oscillate gently as a cradle. Now, singing yet more freely, candles burning with a yellow light, come the faithful from the very oldest to the very youngest: from that bent and withered woman whose husband was shot long ago in Mexico, and whose five children died in one month from smallpox—from that figure of tragedy to a girl with a permanent wave and ten-cent store pearls; to Concepción, newly waked and stumbling; even to Refugio in Agapita's arms. They all come to adore, to kiss the foot, perhaps the hand, rarely the lips of the naked

Baby Jesus. At the very last the workers from the kitchen. Graciana, a red cloth thrown over her head, falls to her knees at the door and thus approaches most humbly, most devoutly. The poor house, the gleaming *Nacimiento,* songs of reverent folks, two black figures cradling the Child.

When every member of this various company has adored, Felicidad uses the perfume that remains to wash the lipstick off the Baby, swaddles him in fine lace and lays him in his cradle. Polycarpo mounts to set him in his place between Mary and Joseph among the treasures of the shrine. Then they pass trays of nuts and sweets, urging all to partake freely.

Now, toward three in the morning, the hour of dinner is come. Graciana is at the threshold to bid a chosen eight to table. They troop by the cold stove, through the sparse little store, to a small, bare-floored room with saints looking down from faded walls, where a lace-covered table laid with Haviland cups and milky blue glass awaits them. They move deliberately although they have fasted all the day and they are about to be served such food as they rarely see. When they have eaten, exchanging amenities but without waste of time, they are succeeded by another eight, and yet another—at three o'clock and four o'clock and five o'clock happy groups will still be dining at the bounty of the Reyes.

Before the winter morning pales, the slow morning of late December, these good folk have celebrated their Christmas day; they have brought fair Mary to her resting place, they have assisted at the Mass, they have adored the Child and laid him in his silver cradle; they have dined like kings, and all night long they have commingled with their fellows. Hearts warm and spirits glowing, they move away, one family in a shiny car, another in a jalopy of incredible age and decrepitude; by far the greater number on foot, trudging through a graying world perhaps to a house in the next block, perhaps to a bare *colonia* within sound and smell of the stockyards not far away; Polycarpo and Felicidad, with children sleeping and children trailing, back to their own door.

Candlemas, which falls on February the second, is the other great event in Graciana's year. Again the faded red house glows with welcome. Again the people flock in, most of them from the church of Jesús y María where they have witnessed the ceremony of *la levantada,* the taking up of the Christ Child from the manger. Now they are coming here to see the act repeated not by priest and acolytes and full-voiced choir, but by simple folk in a humble home. A young *padrino* and *madrina* arrive carrying bags and bundles. Graciana is taken up with savory labors in the kitchen. Magdalena Montemayor, a rosy grandchild in the circle of her arm, leads the service which tonight includes the story of the Presentation in the Temple.

The godparents kneel on either side of a chair on which is set the forty-day-old Jesus; and the godmother, surrendering her candle to a neighbor, lays out an array of fine small garments, lifts the Child from his cradle, and bathes him again with perfume fine. As she dresses him in lace-trimmed drawers, a sheer petticoat, a pink satin frock adorned with blue bows, and blue coat and hood, the company is singing,

The Silver Cradle

Rockaby, Baby,
In the arms of thine own,
Who came to the world
For love of us alone.

Oh, dearest Father,
My God, and my Lord,
Who smiled so cheerfully
While the winter breezes roared.

Rockaby, Baby, . . .

For the Child's small cradle
My heart may well serve,
As I ask forgiveness,
A grace I don't deserve.

Rockaby, Baby, . . .

On rare occasions, once in ten years perhaps, the little Christ is now given into the guardian hands of
Magdalena, and Mary and Joseph are lifted from the
Nacimiento. To the accompaniment of happy singing the
madrina disrobes them down to their shifts, bathes their
faces, shoulders, and arms with perfume, and dresses them
in garments new and lovely—the Virgin in white gown
and cape of Mary blue, her spouse in green robe and
yellow cloak. Their little straw hats, so characteristic a
part of their costume in Mexico, she carefully hangs on
their shoulders. Sweet-smelling, fresh, and fine they are,
this Holy Family, supplying to humble folk the quality
of elegance their own lives lack.

Then the *madrina* sets the Child in a chair cushioned
with lavender velvet, and makes him safe with a silver

cord. The *padrino* arranges a tray of *confites* before him. And in his satin dress, sitting on his velvet pillow, in a room ringing with children's voices, the Baby Jesus is presented for the adoration:

> At dawning of the day
> The little Child was born,
> And that is why we sing
> Our joyous song at morn.
>
> Like robes of silk thy love
> Shall warm thy straw-filled bed.
> Oh, hold me to thy breast!
> Let joy world-wide be spread!

When old and young have paid tribute, the Infant, Mary, and Joseph, are set high above the railroad yard, the swimming pool, the jumble of toys and trinkets, at the very heart of the household shrine.

In the church and in the home, *la levantada* now has been brought to its happy consummation. The *padrino* and *madrina* pass paper bags of sweets, then Graciana appears with her invitation to the feast, a repetition of the grand dinner of Christmas morning. At the lace-covered table laid with Haviland cups and milky blue glass, the guests visit pleasantly. But there is a sense of parting. Toward eleven o'clock they say good-by, they pass into the night. The Méndez make long and affectionate farewells. At last the house is still.

Graciana goes back to the *Nacimiento*, regarding with satisfaction its bright, multitudinous beauties. Then, with a sigh of contented fatigue, she locks away for another year the chiefest of her treasures.

CHAPTER THREE

Babe of Beauty

At this very moment, in a back yard down the way, Doroteo Domínguez is presenting a thousand-year-old mystery play which has as its theme the shepherds' search for the Babe of Beauty.

Now Doroteo is of a more heroic mold than the gentle folk who conserve the silver cradle. Prohibition was for him a golden era. Golden in more ways than one. Not only could he make money, he could engage in enterprises large and dangerous, suitable to his epic temperament. It is true that he spent a good deal of time in prison, but his pride was unscathed, for he was one with the millions in feeling that no sensible man could be expected to honor a law so unnatural. And when the border patrol caught him on a moonless night unloading little knocked-together craft on the banks of the Rio Grande; or receiving half-naked men who had waded across the river with sacks full of bottles on their shoulders; or when officers halted his truck on the Valley highway, confiscated the liquor cached beneath a mask of golden fruit, and took him into custody—when these things happened, Doroteo accepted fate. A prison sentence was only so much time out, and the life has its compensations. It was his family who mourned. Micaela's face went dead. The half-grown boy and girl moved soundlessly about the house. The rooms took on a quality of bleak, cold waiting, with the Infants Jesus (in the house of Doroteo he is twins) chill and naked under their satin cover, not to be taken up until the master should come home again.

Repeated infractions brought some pretty stiff sentences. But Doroteo was on the whole well fed and healthfully worked; and he came out fairer and finer and younger, a superb Lucifer in the ancient nativity play which is his avocation.

He has held to *Los Pastores* through good times and hard. There have been years that were hard indeed. People get their liquor at a package store now, and green beer drunk in a Mexican kitchen with giant cockroaches adorning the wall is no longer an adventure. Then, the low stone house which was his castle for so many years (rented to be sure) was torn down by order of the Health Department before vermin could finish the job. Doroteo was for a time sadly reduced. He had no occupation that

satisfied his needs, no home that gave a sense of continuity
to his undertakings. One bitter year he went through the
streets peddling ice cream on summer mornings. Luzbel,
Prince of Devils, trafficking in pennies and nickels with
children! It was tragically unfitting. It was so unfitting
that it couldn't last. He was clapped into jail charged with
selling stolen property—six hens and a rooster. His friends
were indignant. "Everybody knows that Doroteo never
did a thing like *that*," they said, holding in contempt the
pettiness of the enterprise. It might have been a serious
business, for the passing of thieved livestock is a major
offense in Texas, but apparently nothing came of the
charges. By what mark do you know that a fowl has been
stolen? Doroteo was out pretty soon and moving in a
larger sphere.

He conceived the idea of convoying laborers to the beet
fields of Michigan. Their departure was a sight to see: the
light of late afternoon, three big trucks drawn up on the
grass-grown space behind the Inn of the Moon; families
loading food and pots and pans and blankets; children
running and leaping at play; Doroteo going from place
to place planning, checking, directing—a nearly silent
man who somehow got things done. Finally they rolled
away with a flourish, trucks full of singing Mexicans
driving out into the night. Doroteo has always said they
were well paid and fairly treated, but he has never repeated the venture.

He has settled down to hauling quite legal freight to
nearby towns. It isn't much of a life but it serves. Then,
too, after much effort and long wandering he and his
wife, the patient Micaela, have found a house set some-

what apart so that their lives are not immediately under the eyes and ears of their neighbors, with space behind for Doroteo to rehearse and to produce his Christmas play. That was essential. For what the songs and processions of *Las Posadas* are to Graciana, what the dancing of Los Chichimecas is to Jesús, of the little matachinas to old Damaso, that *Los Pastores* is to Doroteo Domínguez.

It is, however, a passion and a possession by no means exclusive to him. At least four other Mexicans here in San Antonio treasure, as he does, a manuscript written out in a fair hand in an old ledger. Considering the manner in which the play has been transmitted it is inevitable that the Spanish shall be corrupt, that versions shall vary. And it is unimportant. Doroteo set down crudely parts of *Los Pastores* as it was presented in the towns and country districts of San Luis Potosí, and afterward he paid a man to copy them in a book. Sacramento Grimaldo, the able First Shepherd, learned the play in a village near San Antonio, and being a man of monumental memory he committed it to paper in great detail. But his sister helped him, and her husband wrote in some of the songs as he had heard them in communities along the Rio Grande. When this group coalesced with that of Doroteo Domínguez, the shepherds adhered to Sacramento's text, while the devils followed Doroteo's "book." Thus we have a single company using two manuscripts written down by no less than six variously literate hands!

Santos Esparza, a rather roisterous fellow involved now and then with the law, inscribed the play from memory when a cousin, "although he had no right," took the family manuscript away. Old Salvador, who used to

peddle sweets from a buggy marked *Amigo de los Niños,*
copied it when he was a boy of fourteen or so from the
book of his particular director in the town of Irapuato—
some of it he just remembered. A priest long interested in
folklore has sponsored the translating and printing of a
much reduced version of this manuscript, with language
purified and details transposed in the cause of logic. And
he has not only organized but aided a richly costumed
group of players. Esperanza Arias has abbreviated her
grandfather's "book" to meet the capacity of a charming
company of young girls and children. Thus it comes
about that every year a group of Mexican laboring folk,
sometimes several groups, produces in this Texas town a
mystery play that was old when Joan of Arc was burned
in Rouen market place.

The stories of the various *directores* are much the same.
They are aging men with whom *Los Pastores* goes behind memory; they heard it in their mothers' arms; at
three or four they were, perhaps, young devils trailing
devil fathers; at eight or nine they took the role of the
Archangel Michael. They progressed through minor parts
until, due to dramatic gift, a fine voice, energy, and some
organizing ability, they became Lucifers in their own
right, each with his company of working men trans-
formed for the ends of art into gay shepherds and black
devils terrible to see. Doroteo played as a lad with a group
in his native village. And he played with other groups
thereabouts—men of the piety and simplicity of those to
whom the Herald Angels sang. With his dark, idol's face,
his dramatic presence, his sure sense of rhythm, he must
have been marked even then for a stellar role.

When he came to San Antonio he was already in his thirties. The thing was in his blood. So in the course of time he got together a band of carpenters, bakers, gardeners, country folk from Sacramento's village fourteen miles away—Mexicans who earn poor livelihoods in poor ways, whose common denominator is a devotion to God and to drama.

Men on this level are concerned with no bloodless preservation of the past. Except for the essential core of action anything may be, anything is, changed at will. That is why *Los Pastores* lives and leaps and flickers. The play descends, however, in an antique line. Its progenitors are the Old Testament prophecies, the gospel according to St. Luke, and the many beliefs of a savior born of a virgin that lie behind the scriptural story. Specifically it is an offshoot, however humble, of the liturgical drama of the Roman church. Early in the ninth century a monk at St. Gall, Tutilio was his name, created for already existing music an Easter trope, "Quem quaeritis in sepulchro, christocolae?" And a little later he evolved a similar Christmas trope, "Quem quaeritis in praesepe, pastores, dicite?"

These choral enrichments of the Mass, developing in dialogue form were, scholars say, the fountainhead of drama in the West. In any event there appeared in Rouen, between 1070 and 1100 it is thought, an embryonic play which had for content the tidings to the shepherds who watched by night, the search for the Christ Child, and the adoration at the manger. Canons or vicars, advancing to a crib set up behind the altar were met by priests, *quasi obstetrices,* who asked, "Whom do you seek in the manger, say, O shepherds?"

The play that we see in Doroteo's back yard was born, then, in the mountains of Switzerland, and on the plain of northern France was it fostered. But to the new world it was channeled, of course, through Spain. French priests who treked across the Pyrenees in the eleventh century are believed to have brought with them the drama, or at the very least the idea of drama, of the great religious houses of the north. What these ambassadors of faith accomplished no man knows. Or knows much. For there followed the three-hundred-year blank in Spanish drama. Evidence exists, however, more by what was interdicted than by what was recorded, that plays were presented during that long period: plays secular and plays religious; plays in the country, plays in villages and great cities. And the Golden Age was already gleaming when the Twelve Apostles of Mexico (brown-robed Franciscans) came in the spring of 1524 to save this wild new world of ours.

Perhaps some friar put a manuscript into such luggage as a friar possesses. Certainly the missionaries carried more or less precisely in their heads the religious plays of their homeland. But seeded among primitive people, *Los Pastores* was called upon to repeat history: it must go back, back to its very beginnings, before it could again go forward. The Spaniards found the Indians celebrating in the month of December a great feast in honor of Tonantzín, the Earth Mother—the goddess being represented as "a child coming down from heaven." They took advantage, as the Church has always and everywhere taken advantage, of concurring dates, and soon the Indians "were coming from very far" to celebrate on December twenty-fifth the birth of the God-Child. They shot arrows, they made bonfires, they offered dances and songs. To whom? They hardly knew. They little cared. But when they went into the church for midnight Mass, they found "a gate and a cradle so as to represent Bethlehem, Mary, Joseph and the shepherds." A contemporary writes that "our Lord was willing to receive gifts of these poor and rude shepherds who offered them and their songs of praise with spiritual felicity."

The priests eventually were able to present a complete Christmas cycle, beginning with the angel's message to Zaccharias, continuing through the annunciation to the Virgin and the shepherds' pilgrimage, and culminating in the coming of the Magi. Of this tetralogy it is the story of the shepherds—perhaps because it permits a broader treatment and lends itself more readily to secularization —which has persisted. The natives liked that little play. They liked it so much that they made it their own. They introduced dialogue and dancing and business pleasing to themselves. They added to and they subtracted from the priests' drama, they achieved an affair so gay and roister-ous, so little ritualistic, that in 1585 it was forbidden in the church—after which it was given outside. It was taken over then by the people, and it has passed from un-lettered Mexican to unlettered Mexican for 350 unbroken years.

Of formal history the play has none. But from the Gothic churches of France to the plateresque piles of Spain, to the sun-washed adobes of Mexico, to the frame homes of poor Mexicans in San Antonio, the nucleus has remained the same: the shepherds' search for the Babe of Beauty. To make such a theme dramatic, there must, of course, be struggle; and evil is the natural enemy of good. Very early devils appeared, and as everywhere in literature the soldiers of Satan are more vital, more compelling, than the men of good will. From tension, even monotony, there must be relief, so a hermit out of Spanish drama is encouraged to make his part as funny as he is able. Gila and Bato, a traditional, homely pair, are introduced, but Bato's role is transferred to another shepherd, Bartolo. There are long references to Old Testament characters and prophecies. There are passages from Calderón, there is a song from Góngora. These observations do nothing toward establishing the authorship of the play, but they do prove that ritual in process of becoming drama has been handled by the minds of men who knew Calderón and Góngora. And the Bible.

It is not, however, with St. Gall in the ninth century, nor with Rouen in the eleventh, nor with Mexico in the sixteenth, but with San Antonio in the twentieth, that we are here concerned. One night in the fall of the year Doroteo and the children, Benito and José María, clear a space in the cluttered back yard, putting aside the chicken coops, penning the geese, securing the lamb, and backing the truck into the street, for the *compañeros* are coming every week now to rehearse the shepherds' play. Old men there are, sturdy fellows in their prime, gay blades, two children. Some of them have been singing these songs all their lives, some of them are learning the words tonight. More than one has come to fulfill a *promesa* (in this instance a vow to appear in *Los Pastores,* which is, of course, an act of devotion), and all of them are here because they like playing and singing and being together.

The troupe, with women and children in attendance, assembles with incredible regularity and incredible promptitude. Benito places on a small table a religious picture, any religious picture, and supports it with an empty beer bottle. The shepherds march in singing. With this portion of the play the Domínguez concern themselves not at all. It is exclusively in the hands of the First Shepherd, Sacramento Grimaldo, an unpretending man whose place is nevertheless the head of the table. He guides the children. He prompts from memory his brother, his brothers-in-law, his nephews, his small niece, any actor who hesitates—even, on rare occasions, Doroteo himself. Where Sacramento is needed, Sacramento is there. When the devils appear José María takes over as faithful and efficient mentor. She and Sacramento are watchful that every actor shall know his part, take his cue. With direction they concern themselves not at all. The traditional business is well established, and beyond that everyone's role is his own affair. As the evening advances, as they come to the parts they like best, the men sing more freely, little boys abet their devil fathers, women join in the shepherds' songs. The scene takes on a quality of charm: a mass of low buildings, stark tree trunks, men, women, and children singing under the stars.

Now *Los Pastores* is an affair flexible in the extreme. Successive generations cut the text to accord with the capacity of the players and the temper of the audience, the tendency being to sacrifice theology to humor. The

cast likewise varies. If Sacramento hasn't twelve shepherds, he can do with ten. While now and then if Doroteo
is shorthanded, a smooth-cheeked, pink-coated young
pastor stands singing with the devils. One company includes a cowboy of the western plains; another introduces
Herod majestic in pink cambric, and the Three Kings attended by elegant small pages. The necessity is that *Los
Pastores* shall be produced, the urge for drama expressed,
the sense of devotion satisfied.

During the days before Christmas, just at the time
when Graciana is occupied with her vast *Nacimiento* and
the celebration of *Las Posadas,* the women of the *Pastores*
players are busy with their own tasks. Dionicia who has a
family of nine to tend and feed and love is outfitting the
Archangel Michael, aged eleven, with short lavender
pants, white skirt and cape, paper wings and silver crown.
Pilar is renovating the white dress worn by small Gila,
daughter to one of the shepherds and cook for the expedition, covering a hat with the same stuff, and refurbishing
a staff surmounted by a stylized tin bird. The hermit's son
has created a mask of canvas with simplified features,
goatskin hair, and long plait of rope, and his daughter is
sewing crimson and yellow patches on an old gray bath-
robe. The wives and mothers of the shepherds are making
coats of pink muslin, one or two of green, and covering
sombreros turned up in Gainsborough fashion with satin
or with tissue paper, or simply decking them with tinsel
and ribbons and flowers. They are fashioning or freshen-
ing the little beaded and embroidered satchels which each
man wears at his side in token that he is a traveler. The
women of the captains of the shepherds have only to

attach colored streamers to tambourines; but the others are devising or renewing gay, colorful staffs which have not one crook but five converging into a sort of crown from which many little bells depend. They are decorating them with multicolored tissue paper, with ribbons and flowers and Christmas finery, surmounting one with a white bird, another with a silver star. In the more creative aspects of this work, the men themselves occasionally take a hand. A shepherd may evolve a pink and yellow melon which opens and closes at the pull of a cord; another may build a boat of cardboard and tissue paper, or a little room in which the Holy Family is assembled. It matters only that the staffs shall be gay and tinkling.

The devils' wives, although they are not idle, still have work to do. Micaela is putting in order the Luzbel costume which her lord has worn through three decades: a great cape all black and rose, a beaded apron, a breastplate of small mirrors, a pearl-encrusted and mirror-studded crown from which tall plumes ascend. The women of the lesser demons are sewing red braid on black suits, or unpacking capes adorned with crescents and gold stars. Most of the masks are created by an old tinsmith "who knows how," and they endure from year to year. They represent, or at least suggest, animal heads, some with great frightening teeth, some with wide open red jaws from which horrid tongues hang out, one with merely the smug look of seeming sin. The devils are always completely costumed—perhaps in life as in art they are creatures of more force than the servants of God. But the shepherds, even for the dress rehearsal of December twenty-third, even for the *première* of Christmas Eve, are never altogether ready. A few of them lack jackets or decorated hats; one, or possibly three, a crook. These deficiencies are likely to be eliminated, or at least alleviated, as the weeks pass. If *Los Pastores* continued through the spring it might be a completely costumed production, but it runs, officially, only from December twenty-fourth through February second, the ritualistic performances taking place on Christmas Eve, Epiphany, and Candlemas.

The season opens and closes, if that be expedient, at the home of the leader. So a few days before Christmas Doroteo and Benito bring out one of those great mahogany frames which formed the background for old-fashioned bars. It is a pity that the mirror is lacking, for with it the scene would gain in mystery and depth. Such as it is, however, they attach the heavy frame to the back of the house beneath an overhanging roof, and place before it a narrow table. In the missing mirror space they arrange a young forest of greenery. They string small lights through the branches, high above all they hang a large one, wholly unshaded. And climbing on a ladder this Mexican peasant who can barely read and write fastens at the very top a scroll which proclaims in letters of gold, *Gloria in Excelsis Deo.*

Then the women take over the business of complicating their precious crib. It is neither so large nor so elaborate as the *Nacimiento* of Graciana, nor so churchly as that of the Rodríguez, but it is nevertheless an achievement. Near the center they place the ox—a bull straight from the ring, blood oozing from his nostrils, and a *banderilla* in his shoulder. Beside him they set the patient ass, not far away the shepherds. They dispose where they can sheep and deer, the cock that crowed with joy, any animals whatsoever. Then they fill the available space with a litter of objects, with vases and baubles and shells, with models of a filling station and of the shrine of Guadalupe, with a decorated wasp's nest, Christ crucified on a cross of blue glass, and a figure of Buddha. They do all that they know, and every year something different, to make their crib lovely. Then Doroteo covers the whole with a protecting canvas and they wait.

But not with folded hands. Micaela and José María have still much housewifely work to accomplish, for the players will dress in one of the rooms and the whole place will be overrun with people. On Christmas Eve they are occupied to capacity with cooking; they make mountains of tamales, sometimes with sugar and raisins added; or, rarely, Micaela may decide on *buñuelos*—flat, round pastries fried in deep fat. These are a task indeed. Women come in to help with limitless tortillas, and Benito brings the ingredients for gallons of coffee. Normally they prepare for twenty-three players and their families, and their own closest friends. But in a year of great prosperity, they may invite all and sundry.

Doroteo has made on the previous day complete preparations for the dress rehearsal which itself attracted a considerable crowd. So on Christmas Eve he and Benito have only to bring out the figures of Mary and Joseph, and the women to come with the twins called Jesus—for Micaela possesses a figure of the Holy Child, as does her mother, and one may not take precedence over the other. Then Doroteo sets up the devils' lair, a canvas cubicle with the praying hermit, Michael, and the conquered Lucifer on the flaps; and with the help of Benito places some backless benches, not before, but at right angles to, the *Nacimiento*. Thus they face each other across a narrow aisle which is the stage. The result of such an arrangement is that the people who have what are considered the best seats, the places of honor near the crib, are in the midst of the singing and much of the time behind the shepherds, while those at the farther end are intermittently in danger of being knocked over by onrushing devils. But that is of small moment. Wherever you sit or stand, somebody is suddenly before you, and a hundred bodies are pressing on your back. *Los Pastores* is an intimate and an exhausting experience.

Before night falls the animals are penned up, but they still are present. Hens cluck worriedly. The lamb bleats protest. An occasional goose flaps his white way down the aisle. Suddenly the place is bright. Neighbors are coming with their chairs, setting them where they can. A truck draws up, packed with Damaso's family in from the farm. People of every age and many conditions are arriving. Great-grandmothers are being helped to their places, grandmothers are rolling their own, mothers are quieting their babies with pacifier, bottle, or breast. Carmens are whispering together; young men are combing their shining hair. A laborer in jeans and a wide hat guides a line of children and a slender wife wrapped in her shawl and her dignity. A little boy in blue coat and full red trousers, somehow suggesting Goya, leans and eventually sleeps against a black skirt. Smiling, ragged urchins climb to uncertain roofs, perch in the branches of tall trees. There is a very occasional drunk whom Doroteo with determina-

tion and quite without fanfare gets rid of, a more occasional party of priests whom he ceremoniously conducts
to a box arranged for them near the crib. There are a great
many people in this small back yard. There is a sense of
gaiety, but there is neither noise nor confusion. Doroteo
a black figure with face in shadow under a great hat,
goes about preoccupied, speaking rarely. He has respon-
sibility, he has authority. And this is his First Night.

That crowded small space, those dark-faced, tranquil
people, that focus of light and devotion, the gleaming
Nacimiento. The sound of many small bells. Gila beside
the Crib. Enter ten singing shepherds with tinkling, gay
crooks. The Archangel Michael escorted by the captains
of the shepherds jingling their tambourines. The old
masked hermit with long rosary of spools. They kneel,
still singing. Then the small girl, coming down between
the rows of tinseled men, takes her place beside the winged
boy.

Now it must be understood that the children are not in
the scene which follows Michael and Gila, the archangel
and the cook. They are Mary and Joseph wandering dis-
consolate in Bethlehem. Overwhelmingly assisted by the
captains of the shepherds, Parrado and Tebano, they sing
the *posada* songs, hard, dragging pleas for shelter. The
remaining *pastores,* all ten of them, are the master of the
inn, first refusing, finally granting permission to enter.
Then the Holy Pilgrims come forward and the company
kneels, singing, before the crib.

Las Posadas being thus disposed of, *Los Pastores* begins.
Parrado has already received tidings of the Child new-

born. But he has lost the way, he does not know whom to
ask where is the road that leads to the manger.

His companions, Tebano, Naval, Toringo, Lizardo,
Cucharón, Melicio, Mengo, Julio, Gerardo, Bato, and
Bartolo, reassure him:

> Be not disturbed shepherd,
> Be not thy thoughts wild;
> Thy steps shall be guided
> To the newly born child.

After endless talk, they set out on their quest. And
somewhere on the way they sing:

> Within Bethlehem's gate
> Is divine clarity,
> For a saviour is born
> To bring liberty.
> To Bethlehem's gate
> We journey with mirth
> And Gila's tamales
> Toward this happy birth.

The last stanza expresses the theme of the play:

> War, War we shall give him,
> And war we must give,
> To hell and the demon
> While we tremblingly live.

Then, with a change of melody:

> To do good to man
> At the same time was seen

The Silver Cradle

The rose of Jericho,
The wheat of Bethlehem.

On this benign note great Luzbel takes the stage. A magnificent figure with plumed crown and drawn sword, his face half-hidden by a silver-spangled veil, he speaks in tones that roll and thunder. The birds, the flowers, the stars in their sudden changes, together with his own agony, tell him that the birth of the Redeemer is at hand.

He issues a call to his cohorts. Black and red devils wearing horrendous masks dash in to the popping and flashing and smoking of firecrackers thrown in their path. Luzbel reads from a scroll the ancient prophecies of a child to be born of a virgin. Although he foresees his own downfall he is determined to fight a good fight. "Gather for war," he cries, "war against man." The black band pledges faith and follows him into outer darkness.

Again the voices of shepherds singing in the hills:

At night, when the moon shines bright,
And by day, 'neath the sun's hot ray,
Snare the birds, snare the finch and the
    sparrow,
To sing in the church to-morrow.

Miguel announces that Christ, "the source of life," is born.

Enter heavy-browed Luzbel. And there follows the first struggle between the demon bent on destroying "that woman and her Child," and the angel whose mission it is to protect "the rose of Jericho, the wheat of Bethlehem."

Swords flash and threats fly back and forth. But the duel is inconclusive. Miguel retires, not to a cloud but to a

[58]

kitchen chair, declaring that he has come to earth to con-
quer Luzbel. Then the Force for Good, making a colorful pile of hats and crowns and tambourines, surrendering
crooks to women sitting near the crib, troops into the
house for supper.

Evil takes the field. Luzbel calls in his aids: Satanás,
Pecado, Astucia, Asmodeo, Barrabás and Beelzebub.
These frightful creatures run on one by one, cross swords
and go into conference around the council table.

There is much dramatic talk, much pointing of swords
toward heaven. Pecado reads with lengthy comment the
list of the Seven Deadly Sins which, spread through the
earth, will surely send mortal man to hell for all eternity.
The speeches are punctuated by singing and moaning and
groaning, by malign laughing and heartbroken wailing
—taken up by children sitting on the earth and by boys
clinging to bare tree limbs. The satanic crew declares war
against man and against God, marches around singing,
and with a final clashing of swords departs.

Now comes, on the great feasts and occasionally on
days less significant, an intermission. The players form
two lines down the narrow stage, the devils and the hermit
take off their masks, and the *madrinas* appear. More than
one woman has brought a costly decoration, a broad ribbon embroidered, beaded, or flowered, which she passes
like an order across the chest of a favorite player. Doroteo
is always several times honored, as is Sacramento Grimaldo. These actors receive only their due, for they carry
the weight of the production. Then the *madrinas* move
down the lines with baskets or trays, dropping into the
hands or held-open pockets of the players candy and pop-

corn, fruit and animal crackers. The men are as pleased as children.

The action is taken up by Gila, telling the shepherds that they must be on their way.

Led by Miguel and Gila they march around singing:

> To the song
> Of nightingales
> March along
> Across the vales.
>
> With light steps
> Wearily we go
> To see the Messiah
> Born in straw.
>
> Brothers, *pastores,*
> Sister dear,
> We make our way
> Down pathways drear.

Coming to a pleasant pasture and a good spring, the men decide to rest and sup. There is no camp, there is no fire, there is no supper. They are where they have been throughout the evening, in the aisle leading to the *Nacimiento.* But they do take off their satchels, and they do squat. Luzbel enters and engages the hermit in a comic interlude; then he denounces the old man to the shepherds but, it being revealed that El Hermitaño also seeks St. Mary's Boy, the *pastores* invite him to journey with them.

There is interminable speaking and singing. Satanás tries to discourage the travelers with tales of the dangers and hardships of the way, to lure them with promises of food, warmth, and riches. And Luzbel, failing with all his subtle art to win them, issues dreadful threats.

Miguel appears, to give once more the joyful news, but first to banish his great enemy. Now the definitive struggle between the fierce Force for Evil and the tender Messenger of Light. Luzbel, realizing at last that this is the archangel who hurled him down from heaven, that Mary is the Lady whom Isaiah promised, finally succumbs.

Prostrate before the *Nacimiento,* small Miguel's foot on his shoulder, he pours forth rhythmic oratory confessing his sins and recalling his former greatness. The speech is punctuated by shepherds singing:

> Listen sweet flowers to me
> How unlike today is the past.
> Last eve mortals marveled at me
> But now shades circle me fast.

The six frightful devils dash to the rescue. Joining hands they form a chain, and moaning and wailing they try with all their might, but unavailingly, to raise great Luzbel from the earth.

It is only when Miguel relents, telling his adversary to go where he will be seen no more, that the conquered prince arises. The satanic aids return, cross swords, and deliver themselves of their final speeches. Then they march around singing, and depart with a well-placed confidence in their continuing power.

The conflict now is ended. The whole tone of *Los Pastores* lightens, lifts, as the shepherds sing:

The heavens are chanting "Victory,
Saint Michael has prevailed!"
Watch Lucifer crestfallen flee,
His baneful schemes unveiled!

They march and sing. They sing and march. After the trials and dangers of the way they come at last to Bethlehem, to the crib before which all the story of the play is enacted.

Tebano, being the eldest, is given the privilege of first adoring. He and Parrado approach singing, and Tebano kneels to present to "most sacred virgin Mary" a basket filled with flowers.

Gila offers her best, a little dance, a little song, and a "humble gift of linen sheets and pillow cases."

Now El Hermitaño, something loath. After him the shepherds with songs and praise and presents. Mengo's voice rises:

Upon the star-path
Let me go to Bethlehem

And take these little spoons
To give the newborn child.

Bato brings a decorated wasp's nest, the wild honeycomb found in the mountains yesterday, called for by the text.

Only Bartolo, the lazy one, seriously resists. Melicio pleads,

Come Bartolo, come and see
The slow ass eating hay.

Babe of Beauty

To this he answers,

> I do not care to watch a feast
> When nothing comes my way.

There is stanza after stanza of urging and refusing. Another shepherd, Cucharón, coaxes,

> In Bethlehem is fire-water
> White wine and good mescal.

Bartolo at last relents,

> Now I will get up,
> Because I want to get drunk.

Still singing, his fellows hoist him with poles, and the reluctant shepherd goes forward to make his offerings of milk and honey.

All this is lovely, but the attention of the people is wandering. They are intrigued by a new figure that has appeared at the far end of the yard. Suddenly an Indian dancer leaps into the picture. He wears a buckskin suit, a feather headdress and a black veil, and he carries a bow and arrow. He speaks, he prays. To the music of Doroteo's accordion he moves through a thudding ceremonial dance. With a final genuflection he is gone. The spectators are enchanted.

Parrado takes over, suggesting that they sing a lullaby to the newborn child. The shepherds remove their satchels, hook each two together by their wide ribbons, and swinging them gently as little cradles, raise happy voices:

> Now he sleeps, the babe of beauty,
> Now he sleeps with gracious air,

While he sleeps, let rest come to me
From all my pain and care.

Now he sleeps, the babe of beauty,
Now he sleeps Redeemer small,
"*A la rorro*" sing we to Him,
"*A la rorro*, Lord of all."

Now has come the eternal father,
Now has come the eternal light.
Mary's child has come to bless us,
Jesus is a name of might.

Then the lovely adoration, the last for which the first
was made. The *madrina* distributes candles and sets a tray
of *confites* before the crib. She and her husband kneel,
the woman to undress the small figures and to hang their
garments on the green boughs beside her. Each holding
a lighted taper, they present the naked babies to the long
wandering pilgrims. Gila, the hermit, all the weary shepherds, approach to touch with reverent lips those small
"lambs of God." After them the pious company: mothers
with infants in their arms, ancient women wrapped in
shawls, workmen poor and patched, soldiers wearing on
their chests the ribbons of foreign fields. The priests, if
any came, long since have slipped away. Lads drop down
from roofs and trees. Children are lifted to kiss a small
foot. A girl of perhaps ten years extends slender hands,
looks quickly like a little bird from right to left and,
greatly daring, brushes lightly "the little coral mouth."
  While the people come so reverently, so devoutly, to
the adoration, the spangled shepherds still are singing:

Approach, approach, oh, sinner,
Approach with gladdened heart and hope,
And worship here the newborn child
That just from heaven has arrived.

Look, trembling from the wintry blast
And dolorously crying,
In gentle Mary's sweet embrace
You'll see our holy Saviour.

Oh, come, oh, come, oh, sinner
Oh, come with light and happy heart,
Come to adore the newborn child
In gentle Mary's sweet embrace.

When all the assemblage has adored and partaken of the candy the Infants are laid in their cradle and over them is spread a coverlet of creamy satin.

The shepherds sing and speak and march, they march and speak and sing. They make their farewell farewells. They kneel, still singing. Tebano says the final *adiós*, invoking the Virgin of Guadalupe. *"Viva,"* cry the *hermanos pastores,* and rising they disband.

All through the adoration the people are slipping away. Doroteo goes about the business of covering the *Nacimiento,* of putting out the lights, of locking the gate of his domain. He is abstracted, he is uplifted, he serves God and Art tonight.

Between Christmas Eve and Candlemas the players will go to any home or church to which they may be invited— and not by bitterest cold are they discouraged. They may be received in the back yard of a poor house over beyond the cemetery on an evening when a shrewd wind rocks the *Nacimiento,* flutters the crooks, blows off the shepherds' hats, and carries the voices down the narrow streets of the quarter. They may appear in the parish hall of the church of Jesús y María. There they find the traditional arrangements, for the nuns have the good judgment to disregard the stage, to set the *Nacimiento* on the floor, and to arrange the seats in the customary manner. But the entrance is led by a dark, slant-eyed Mary of perhaps four years, and a small, black-bearded Joseph with blossoming staff. They genuflect with the accustomed piety, the natural grace, of Mexican children. Then they are lifted to places high on either side of the crib, and soon their eyelids droop. Through praise and prayer and conflict, they are sweetly sleeping.

Or the *compañeros* may go far out on the edge of town where they play in a yard full of woodpiles and haystacks, with the odor of pigs and incense contending in the air. The place is dimly lit with oil lamps and lanterns. Near the dressing room a fire blazes, flame and shadow dramatizing the faces of shepherds and devils and plain people. The *Nacimiento* is of the simplest, a shelter of boughs on which hang the small garments, the pants and skirt, the dress and cap and cape of the Baby Jesus. The sky is low, the stars are many. The yard is thick with tranquil Mexicans. There is quietude, there is an ambiance of happiness. Except for the distant glow of San Antonio, this might be some far country place.

On February second the season comes to its official end. But if attractive invitations are presented, if men are not working, if Sacramento wishes to honor his aged mother, it may be continued through succeeding weeks. It may be continued even into spring. Why stop playing ever? In any event, on Candlemas the troupe comes again to the home of Doroteo Domínguez. *Los Pastores* is on that night an affair of especial brilliance. The *Nacimiento* glows with many lights. The crowd is large and expectant. The players are gay, they are free, they are well into their parts. Doroteo is confidently at ease. It may not be said that his periods are richer, more rounded; they are always superlative. But firecrackers in more than usual numbers pop in the path of the lesser devils. Satanás, Pecado, Astucia, Asmodeo, Barrabás and Beelzebub jump more agilely, wail more mournfully, than ever. Sacramento Grimaldo is not only an actor but a presence, the shepherds feel that all is well. They sing joyously; shaking their gay crooks they let themselves go—particularly the visiting *pastor* with a flask on his hip and his coat revealingly hitched. Micaela outdoes herself in the matter of food, serving that ultimate luxury, *buñuelos*. The *madrinas* bring candy in quantity, decorations most lavish. As always, *Los Pastores* is characterized by monotony, by gaiety, by devotion. But tonight there is a poignancy of happiness, a sense of something lovely coming to its lovely culmination.

This is, of course, the night of the taking up of the little Jesus. When all the company has adored, the *madrina* gives her candle into the keeping of her little daughter. The men are singing freely as she lifts the Infants from their cradle, dresses them in filmy robes, puts hoods on their heads, and laces sandals on their feet with scarlet ribbons. One little figure she sets in his chair, the other she stands at the center of the crib.

Again the *pastores* kneel—with them now is dramatic Doroteo, no longer Prince of Devils, but a black-browed peasant mantled in devotion.

Again the night is full of song:

> Oh, Jesus, Mary, hail to thee
> And Joseph, patriarch, to thee,
> Long live the sacred mystery,
> Long live the holy trinity.

> On cold December twenty-four
> The fine, proud cockerel crew
> With voice as clear as martial horn,
> "Today is born the saviour."

> And Joseph, too, the patriarch,
> Adored the newborn saviour,
> And after dawn had warmed the world
> He kissed the baby's fingers.

The shepherds have come to the end of their journey.

CHAPTER FOUR

The Blessing of the Animals

One day about the middle of January Plutarco Méndez washes the family dog. Felicidad contributes bluing to streak his white coat, and if other coloring matter is at hand he is variously engayed. Then Agapita offers her best ribbon for a bow at his neck. For Cazador is to be taken that afternoon to be blessed, along with other animals of the parish, at the church of Jesús y María.

The ceremony should by rights be performed on the feast of San Antonio de Abad, which falls on January seventeenth but, weather and convenience determining the life of the quarter, it usually takes place on the nearest fine Sunday afternoon. About three o'clock, then, on a bright day of winter, Felicidad and her mother and all the little Méndez, with Plutarco calming an astonished Cazador, join a trickle of friends and neighbors who issue from small, frail houses, drear at this season because they are almost bare of flowers, leading dogs, carrying chickens, struggling with bird cages, guiding goats, and pacifying kittens. Making their way along uneven streets, they pass through the gateway and into the yard of this church which seeks to serve all the needs of its charges.

There is, of course, a time of waiting. A truck rolls in driven by a teenaged lad with his arm thrown about a Belgian police dog; a small girl comes with a bowl of goldfish; children bring boxes of rabbits and baskets of baby chicks; a woman with the reddest of red nails, wearing the greenest of green dresses, is caressing the blackest of black kittens; a very old man holds in his arms his closest friend and companion, a little hairless pelon dog. This is an aggregation of animals disturbing one to another, but being Mexican creatures they are reasonably philosophical. And their guardians at least are content, standing in groups, talking quietly, unhurriedly waiting together.

Now people are drifting into the church, a handful of visitors and perhaps two handfuls of parishioners. Plutarco must stay outside with Cazador, who is barred from explanations—it does not matter, the boy knows well enough why he has come, and the dog would never learn by listening. But Felicidad, little grandmother, and the

The Blessing of the Animals

younger children hear Father Nepo relate, first in Spanish, then in English, the story of San Antonio de Abad, and explain the significance of the ceremony about to be performed. The saint is not to be confused, he says, with Anthony of Padua, who finds lost articles for you, who preached with such peculiar eloquence that he charmed even the stupid fishes. Anthony the Abbot was an Egyptian anchorite of the fourth century, famous in art for the temptations he battled, and in history for the impetus he gave to the monastic life. He became patron of so many homely crafts and creatures—brushmakers, basket weavers, gravediggers, and domestic animals— that he is dear to people who work with their hands and who number among their treasures kittens and hounds and chicks and birds in cages. He is widely known as the patron of hogs, and is usually represented with "a pig for his page." Why this should be is not easy to say unless, as Fuller in his *Worthies of England* quaintly suggests (quoted by Chambers in his *Book of Days*), it is because "being a hermit, and having a cell or hole digged in the earth and having his general repast on roots, he and hogs did in some sort enter-common both in their diet and lodging." In Rome animals are blessed, or used to be, Father Nepo remembers, at the hospital of Sant' Antonio Abbate, down in the Santa Maria Maggiore quarter. The ceremony at one time assumed such proportions that it extended over two or three days, everybody, even the English, wanting to bring their favorite pets or their most useful animals to be sprinkled, sanctified, and placed under the immediate protection of the saint. In the villages of Spain and Mexico the farm animals, oxen, cows, burros and, quite properly, pigs, still are brought decked and garlanded to the church door, and having been duly blessed are led by masters also garlanded 'round the plaza. "It is," the priest says, "a gay sight." The service itself is a manner of giving thanks to God for his benefits, and of asking his blessing on his creatures. All the while the kind father is speaking, there drifts in from without a confusion of low sounds, a suggestion of growling and fluttering and clucking from the waiting beneficiaries.

Now their time approaches. A heavy, black-haired priest, attended by two altar boys, comes into the yard. People who have brought animals form a circle—Anacleto Arrellano, watchman at the church, leading a sleek brown nanny goat; a man managing a lordly ram decorated with green ribbons; Hilaria holding a comfortably clucking hen on one arm, and a white pigeon in a paper sack on the other; a boy stroking a beautiful yellow cat; Cleofas with her lovebirds in a reed cage outlined with pink flowers; a woman with an ancient parrot, his *casa* immaculately cleaned, hung with lace curtains, decorated with pink and rose and purple sweet peas; Pánfila with the white canary from the priests' dining room; the lad with his police dog; gray pigeons touched with rose. People still are coming.

The circle formed, Plutarco occupies himself with maneuvering Cazador into a place where he will receive his full share of holy water and benediction. The priest offers a brief prayer:

"May these animals receive Thy blessing, O Lord, and may it preserve their bodies and save them from all hard-

The Blessing of the Animals

ship. By the intercession of Saint Anthony, through Jesus
Christ Our Lord. Amen."

Then, the little brown boys attending, he moves 'round
the circle dispensing a small rain on trembling creatures.

Quickly the service is finished, slowly the group dis-
perses. Chickens and pigeons are taken back to yards full
of tubs and bottles and derelict automobiles; puppies and
pussies are carried off by pleased children; a small dog
rides away in a basket attached to the handle bars of his
master's bicycle; the nanny goat is led to her tether beside
the church. Plutarco departs with Cazador. But Felicidad
and her mother, Agapita, Juan Bautista, Concepción and
Refugio, stand waiting with others who sense that all is
not yet done.

Among the virtues of the Mexican people, promptness
is not numbered. There remain the unfortunate animals
whose masters, although well-intentioned, somehow have
failed them: whose Ford wouldn't crank; whose clock
was, of course, slow; who took too long in washing and
combing and making ready; who in their very eagerness
to do well finally were found wanting. Boys still are
hurrying up the street with dogs on leashes, women are
coming with arms full of children and chickens, a stout
old dame is struggling with two black goats. As these
poor animals arrive, they meet the blessed departing. It is
evident that the ceremony is ended, but the latecomers do
not turn away. They stand about patiently, hopefully,
even confidently. For although they do not know that the
dark-faced priest who officiated today is the lineal descendant of a saint, they do know that he is kind to all

creatures. Their confidence is well placed. When eight or a dozen animals are assembled, he comes out again, vested and attended, and motions to the waiting hopefuls to follow him to the farther side of the church. They trail along accompanied by a small gallery. The priest pauses at a little tree-shaded enclosure to bless the terrier, the pug, and the mongrel beloved of Father Cruz. Then he moves to the fence which separates the ecclesiastical domain from Eusebia's back yard. There the saintly descendant of a saint bestows holy water and blessing impartially on the washed and the unwashed: on Eusebia's hens pecking in the earth, on her barking hounds, on the two black goats, on a white dog streaked with green, on two minute turtles painted blue and yellow for the occasion. In the doorway stands Eusebia smiling with surprised delight.

The blessing of the animals is now truly accomplished.

CHAPTER FIVE

Apostles Twelve

Anacleto Arrellano is milking a goat by the side of the
church. As with steady rhythm he extracts a foam-
ing quart, he and Polycarpo Méndez are talking—telling
each other, after the manner of humankind, things they
already know.

The twelve apostles will perform their customary acts
of devotion during Holy Week, Polycarpo says. They will
keep a vigil in the church beginning with the seven
o'clock Mass on Maundy Thursday and lasting through
the Mass of the Presanctified on Good Friday morning:

they will present themselves in the chancel for the ceremony of *el lavatorio*; they will lift the dead Christ from his cross and, sorrowing, bear him to his entombment.

Down in the next parish, Anacleto has heard, the apostles will be merry little boys robed in purple. That is true, Polycarpo agrees, but here at the church of Jesús y María they will be as always men, most of them old men, in the Jewish raiment of 2,000 years ago. The same ones who came last year, and the year before, and the year before that, probably will come again this Holy Thursday. But life moves on. People go away. They fall ill. They die. Polycarpo plans to talk within the hour to Amador who, being the oldest of all, has the role of St. Andrew. He will serve this year, perhaps, scarcely another. The processions are not hard, and he could be assisted should the cross prove too heavy. But a twenty-four hour vigil is long for a man nearing ninety.

Father Nepo has charged Polycarpo with the duty of making sure beyond all manner of doubt that not only old Amador, who after all has nothing else to do, but eleven other men are prepared to put aside the affairs of this world—to park their little ice cream carts, to leave their fruit stands, to desert their bars, to take time off from garbage collecting, or lawn mowing or bread peddling—and to devote these hours to the service of their sorrowing Lord. He must take care, too, that their costumes, kerchiefs and draperies of many-colored cambric are complete and in readiness, that the great cross stands waiting. For the ceremonies of the solemnest days of all the year must move with ordered dignity.

A sense of drama and a sense of festival impregnate the

life of the quarter. In the cinema women weep before a presentation of the Passion in which Mary is no delicate ideal but the thickset *mamacita* of a son of thirty. In the church young and old attend to passionate praying and preaching. Outside they buy flowers and herbs and gayly colored cascarones, beverages, and ices. They rest and they visit. Whatever its character, a feast is a feast, an occasion for coming together.

But in the early hours of Thursday morning all is still. Twelve Mexicans pass through the yard of the church with the air of men on some special mission bent. And at seven o'clock there appear in the front pews of the nave twelve Jews—figures with draped heads and flowing garments, blue and yellow and gray and crimson, lavender and green and cream and rose, below which are revealed blue jeans and worn shoes. These are the apostles of Jesus Christ: Peter, James, John and Andrew, Phillip, Bartholomew, Matthew and Thomas, James the son of Alphaeus, Thaddeus, Simon the Canaanite and Judas Iscariot "which also betrayed Him."

Since Passion Sunday the church has been a stark place, and all the holy figures have been shrouded in purple. They still are shrouded. But today the chancel has become a refuge, perhaps a grove of small oaks, perhaps a forest of sweet-smelling cedar. Here are brought costly lilies and tight bouquets from little gardens. Here, tall and fair, flower-laden and candle-lighted, rises the Altar of Repose. To it is carried in solemnest procession the body and blood of Jesus Christ to rest therein the cycle of a day and night. In this green place the apostles keep their vigil, two always kneeling, others waiting to take up the watch. All through the morning there is the quiet coming and going of quiet people. In the flowered chancel hour after hour those immobile figures kneel, apostles who are not heavy lidded, who will not be found sleeping.

At two o'clock, or three o'clock, comes a break. Now is to be commemorated a scene which in other times was enacted by the proudest of the proud ones: by the Catholic kings of England; by the Emperor and the Empress when there were an emperor and an empress in Vienna; by the King and Queen of Spain when they were living out their destiny in tragic splendor. Today the rite is performed by the Pope in Rome, by priests 'round the world, by the Archbishop in the stone cathedral at the heart of San Antonio, by the pastor of this church which serves poor Mexican people. It is *el lavatorio,* the washing of the feet enjoined by Christ on his apostles. Six chairs are set on either side of the chancel, and a table covered with a white cloth and piled with flat, round loaves of bread is placed between them. The twelve apostles seat themselves in the twelve chairs, arranged apparently so that the act shall be experienced rather than observed. Enter the senior priest vested in purple and gold, attended by altar boys carrying the necessities for this act of humility which commemorates that moment in the upper room in Jerusalem when Jesus "putteth water into a basin, and began to wash the feet of the disciples and to wipe them with the towel wherewith he was girded."

And when He said to them, "If then I being your Lord and Master, have washed your feet; you also ought to wash one another's feet.

Apostles Twelve

"For I have given you an example, that as I have done to you, so you do also."

Father Nepo intones the order of the service, kneels, washes, dries, and kisses the foot of one man, passes swiftly to another. Thus is the injunction obeyed with simplicity, expedition, and quietude.

Then, in memory of the supper which they did eat, the priest blesses the loaves, and to each apostle he gives bread. Again the many-colored figures assume their vigil. Through the drowsing hours of the afternoon, through the long chill night, two men kneel unmoving. Dark forms come and go. Mothers soothe their babies. Children sleep in the pews. In the house of Eusebia folk are drinking coffee, making contact, visiting in low tones.

In the church there is the sound of praying people, of people singing. The voices of apostles raised in a wailing, wavering chant. There is silence. Again there is prayer, there is silence, there is song. With the Mass of Good Friday the long watch ends. This is another day, another drama. But in it, also, the apostles serve their Lord.

The hours of the Agony are, of course, the point of high drama in the Christian year. Before a background of faraway village and thunderous sky, Christ is crucified. At the foot of the cross stand figures of the sorrowing mother and young John whom Jesus loved. On a lower level weary apostles wait to express their ultimate devotion. Men and women come early to kneel with arms extended at the chancel gate, to leave the humblest and most abundant flowers of the season, little bouquets and great sheafs of sweet smelling manzanillas.

The Silver Cradle

Long before the appointed hour the church is filled, crowded to the farthest corner, to the highest gallery, to the last chancel step. The pews are packed, the aisles are packed, people are standing along the walls; old women and young children are folding up, if only they can find space, anywhere on the floor. From high-up windows the black-framed faces of nuns look down. There is not an inch in that great hot building in which some Mexican is not worshiping. Brown-skinned, poorly dressed people are standing in the doorways; they have climbed into the arches of the porch; they are crowded into the vestibule, on the steps, down onto the sidewalk, longing but not hoping to enter. Within is a communicable intensity, a sense of devotion—devotion of a quality that mounts to drama.

The gray Christ on his black cross. Eleven apostles waiting. The voice of the priest speaking with passion:

"Father, forgive them, for they know not what they do. . . . Amen I say to thee: this day thou shalt be with me in paradise. . . . Woman, behold thy son. Behold thy mother. . . . My God, My God, why hast thou forsaken me? . . . I thirst. . . . It is consummated. . . . Father, into thy hands I commend my spirit."

Enveloping the words of sorrow, the sad intonation of music repeats the theme.

As the hours move into late afternoon, intensity becomes more tense in that church filled with responding people. A wave of movement, a breath of relief, passes through the multitude. Tension has reached the breaking point. Now comes the release of action. The eleven apostles (Judas has passed forever from the scene) move to take the dead Christ down from the cross. St. James draws from the hand a nail, and kisses the wounded palm. Old St. Andrew, bright-eyed, haggard-faced, too feeble to serve, kneels in devotion. Black-robed women bearing silvered trays have come into the sanctuary. To them are entrusted the crown of thorns, the cruel spikes, as they are drawn from pierced hands and feet. Then is Christ wrapped in his winding sheet and borne along the road to the new tomb in the garden of Joseph of Arimathaea.

Down the aisle Anacleto moves. Crucifer and candle bearers. Old women in black mantillas, the society of the Buena Muerte. The red and green and yellow figure of frail St. Andrew, bending under the weight of the heavy cross. His Greco face is gray and drawn, his eyes are fever bright, he is all but exhausted with long watching. He moves slowly and, too weak to bear alone his burden, is aided by a comrade also old and feeble. Apostles in their many-colored garments marching solemnly. Apostles bearing the wounded Christ, his eyes gray shadowed, marks of the thorns on his blood streaked brow. Black-clad women with the sacred relics. Daughters of Mary. Then the faithful. Out into the pale light of late afternoon the procession passes. The priests have departed from the scene. This is an expression wholly of the people.

There is no background of beauty for these quiet marchers, no delicate cloister arches, no fountain splashing into marble pool, no tall poplars black against the evening sky. There is only a bare beaten yard bordered by church and school and the poor homes of poor people. Around this unlovely space they move, a line of silent figures carrying their dramatic burden. St. Andrew wavers beneath the cross and must be assisted. Around they go again, those old daughters of the Buena Muerte, those apostles with their tenderly beautiful Master, those black-robed women, all those pious people. Polycarpo speaks a low word, and it passes from apostle to apostle. Then the men begin to sing, music from the earth of Mexico, they say, certainly a wailing song of sorrow. On they sadly march, sadly singing. But from the church comes music in another mood: the voices of the people are uplifted, their spirit is triumphant. This is indeed the Good Death, the death which is a victory. Through the door the procession passes, moving up the aisle on conquering waves of sound. Anacleto and his aids relieve the worn apostles of the heavy cross. They lay the broken body on a bier of purple at the chancel steps. From the sacristy men bring palms to embower Christ's resting place; at his head they set his mother swathed in habiliments of woe, and on either side they light white tapers. Now come the apostles to kiss the wounded flesh, the sacred relics. Then they vanish.

The people are pressing forward, so many and so eager that they must be restrained. They move toward the bier to adore, to make offerings, to receive flowers in remembrance. At last the pressure lessens. The surging multitude has satisfied its devotion. The stream of worshipers never ceases, but they come now one by one, or in small family groups: a black-shocked Indian approaches on his knees, his arms extended, his body a cross, and kisses the blood-streaked foot in a very ecstasy of devotion; a blind man led by a very little boy makes his offering and turns away with flowers in his hand. Graciana is there, and aged

Apostles Twelve

Cleofas. Felicidad assists her mother, and Agapita lifts small Refugio to kiss the poor hand. Very late Doroteo comes. Girls in black mantillas leave pale flowers. Small children slip along in twos and threes, wholly reverent; mothers lay the cheeks of young babies against the wounds; a girl with sodden face and shaken body kneels weeping beside the bier, and will not be comforted; many a woman wrapped in a black *rebozo* carries a child in her arms, another not yet seen. They come to adore the dead Master, to offer their love and their pence, these people of an utter poverty who enter here into a field of universal beauty. The lilies are rich and red and many, numberless are the roses. The church is quiet, the arches thick with dusk, flames of candles waver. From somewhere in the shadows a woman's voice rises, old, metallic, hard and tragic; then a man's, a wail of sorrow, the uttermost reach of human desolation. A pause. Figures move silently up the aisle, as silently down to the door. Again the voice rises, and yet again, that last sadness of the human heart.

Then it, too, is still. There remains but the twilight weighted with the scent of flowers, the dead Christ in his winding sheet, living light of candles, human creatures kneeling. When the place is bright, when the priests come back, then come the apostles, too. They carry their Master in procession 'round the yard, they sing again their sorrow.

Silently they melt away, weary and worn and utterly content.

CHAPTER SIX

Easter and Epiphany

Polycarpo and Felicidad Méndez being given to standing, however uncertainly, on their own feet do not find
it necessary to send their children to Pascual's school. It
exists for people poorer and more helpless, but they know
the master well, and they share in many of the activities
of that unassuming good man.

Pascual was president of the Anti-Communist Society
of San Antonio until the group dissolved itself for lack
of visible resistance. And he is principal, janitor, and cook
at a school for children who do not fit into, or cannot get

into, any other institution. His political convictions derive inviolate from Rome and are not here relevant. But his vocation springs from the blend of characteristics and circumstances that directs the destiny of man: from a religious compulsion, from a need to serve, from a scholarly leaning in a not very scholarly Mexican, from poverty and ill health, from the possession of a little house set in a garden.

Now see how all these strands weave together. Pascual has made a vow of service to children, and he lives among families whose progeny, like their needs, are multitudinous. Although he came to San Antonio when he was fifteen and is to some degree a product of the public school system of the town, he is conscious of and distressed by the degradation of manner and manners among his compatriots on the Texas side of the Rio Grande, and by the corruption of the Spanish tongue. He must do something. He does. He has a house which adapts to any purpose, and just enough strength to maintain a school—a school in which he can form conduct, correct language, and overlay life with a patina of religion. This ill man with a respect for learning and an urge to be of use to his fellows teaches poor people in his house and in his garden—English in the morning, Spanish in the afternoon and evening, manners all day long.

The ownership of that small property is of first importance. It is the bedrock, the foundation stone, on which the school as an enduring institution stands. Pascual possesses not only a house but a home, not only a home but a homestead. It represents to him and to his sister, Epifanía, continuity of life. The place is well known. They were there last year and the year before. They carry on with the assurance that they will be there next year and the year after. Perhaps all their lives. For, although taxes do pile up, the state is not a landlord threatening eviction on the first of any month. It is true that the place lies in the line of march of the great housing project, and a solid and sanitary and efficient apartment may one day rise on the site of this charmingly dilapidated school. But that is an eventuality of the future, and Pascual would welcome it. He would be compensated for his holdings, of course, and with money in hand he and Epifanía willingly would seek another little house in another little garden.

In the meantime, all things being relative, they feel that they are fortunate. They have a house, not a shack; a *casa*, not a *jacal*. It has two rooms, both floored, a little porch, a roof which keeps out the water pretty well, and once it was painted. It is set back from the street behind a high picket fence, and a crude arbor on which a trumpet vine clambers leads from gate to doorstep. Tall cottonwood trees rustle with a sound like rain on hot, dry mornings; there are peach and massive fig trees; roses and lemon verbena, jasmine, and those white spidery lilies that suggest the ghosts of witches—these and a hundred flowers beside flourish in disordered confusion. For the garden of Pascual's sister is remarkable in that plants grow not from pots and cans but from the very earth. It is a sweet place, tangled, untended, and heavy-scented.

We find here no refuge of peace withdrawn from the ways of men, but a habitation which serves every sort of human need. In the shade of a great tree is a not very inviting bed where Pascual sleeps on summer nights. Epifanía's washtubs hang on the walls, along with a handbasin and towels and shaving brushes and bird cages and strings of red peppers. People come to ask for food, and Pascual gives what he has; for water, and he supplies what they need; for counsel, and he offers of his selfless best. Men drift in at dusk, among them Polycarpo Méndez, to sit talking and, as they talk, to form with visible effort their political and social opinions. Pascual is there to guide them; behind him stands the parish priest, and farther back, of course, the Pope of Rome. Men come to leave pennies and nickels in the schoolmaster's hand, the eight cents a month which they pay as they can into a medical insurance fund of which he is custodian. The bookkeeping must be a monumental undertaking, for the money is brought in minute amounts and at uncertain intervals. But brought it is, and when one of the beneficiaries, having exhausted his grandmother's knowledge of herbs and charms, and having made a vow to the Lord of the Miracles, badly wants a doctor, he has only to pass through the gate, under the arbor, and knock on the door of the schoolmaster's house. Pascual will get one. Then, if neither faith nor skill avails, the man comes back to draw on the treasury of a sadder society, one which assures the black solemnity of burial. The knowledge that all will be plainly and decently done, and by one's own efforts, that humiliation will not be added to grief—the assurance is a blessed reward for much sacrifice.

Such services are by-products of Pascual's energy. His vocation is the school and the children. They pervade his life, they invade his home. There are classes in the kitchen, there are classes on the porch, there are classes in the garden. Indeed, when the weather is too wet or too cold for outdoor teaching, older pupils may be sent away and the little fellows crowded into that one room. The bare space to the west, used as a runway by two friendly dogs, is also playground and assembly hall. The school assembles only in fine weather.

The second room of the house has somewhat the character of a private apartment. At any rate, Epifanía sleeps there. This woman deserves well of the institution, for she does washing and house cleaning to keep it afloat when the tuition isn't adequate. And considering the system, it isn't likely to be: the parents pay a dime a week, if they have it. To be really useful to people on such an economic level—and that is its aim—Pascual's school must function throughout the year. Many of the parents are employed, irregularly at least, and when a child's mother is from home picking out pecans, or peeling tobacco, or sewing infant's clothes, provision must be made for him through a long day, six days a week, summer and winter alike. A good number of the youngsters who drift into Pascual's garden seem to be ineligible for public, or even for church, schools. The offspring of migrant workers are perpetual misfits because they are taken out of class for months every year. Some of the children lack clothes. Some of them labor under defects of vision or hearing, a slower than average understanding. The master has under his gentle hand some thirty children, and for each one he does the best he can.

On summer mornings Pascual, immaculate in peasants' white, his voice low, his face tranquil, stands in the shade

of a cottonwood tree, eight or ten little boys and girls
on backless benches before him. At his feet sits a small
girl stringing colored beads. With great seriousness, in a
language he fondly imagines to be English, he is telling
the story of the American flag. Then he proceeds to a
lesson, using a Fourth School Reader, Fallon & Co., Dub-
lin and Belfast, 1906, which comprehends, together with
much else, "Elegy Written in a Country Church-Yard,"
"The Harp That Once Through Tara's Halls," Keble on
influence, excerpts from Pickwick; and the chapter on
how Gulliver captured a fleet. In Epifanía's garden boys
and girls with voices of brass intone: "Te lowing 'erd
wind slowly o'er te lea, . . . Te 'arp 'at onze trou Tara's
'als . . ."

What it means to them nobody knows, but they read
very well. On the porch children, disposed among cats
and vegetables and washing arrangements, think about
studying their lessons. In the arbor a boy sits unregarded,
singing.

The kitchen is the schoolroom in chief. It is enlivened
by pictures of notabilities so various as St. Cecelia and
Charlie Chaplin, Francis of Assisi and Napoleon Bona-
parte; furnished on one side with a small iron stove and
equipment for cooking and eating, on the other with a
wicker table, a bench, a blackboard, and a chart on which
an elementary reading lesson is displayed. In the middle of
the room are two rocking chairs in which children sway
happily to and fro. Here a boy of twelve is initiating into
the mysteries of knowledge pupils a little younger than
himself. He is serious but not solemn, and he seems to
have no disciplinary problems. One can learn, apparently,

sitting in a chair that is too high, at a table that is too low, from a teacher who never heard of a degree. This is a class in English. "Go to the window. Open the door," the young instructor says, and at each command a child demonstrates concretely that he understands. They have a story about a prairie dog and they are eager to draw a picture of him. But to pronounce his name! That is a hard one. Teacher can't either. He turns to arithmetic, setting simple problems on the board. His pupils shout the answers. The room is full of eager voices.

Outside the door a dog scratches fleas, a neighbor's radio blares music from Mexico. Oblivious, Epifanía sings as with bucket and dipper she takes water to her garden. Among the flowers, small children play.

In the evening, this casual atmosphere of desultory study vanishes. Then comes an older group to take up the pursuit of knowledge.

For two years Pascual put his plant at the disposal of "the mightiest government on earth," and the WPA sent a young woman to instruct in the elements of reading and writing and citizenship. A class of twenty came five nights a week, and that was considered a fine response. On winter evenings brown-faced men and women crowded into that small kitchen, made bright and warm for their benefit. Certainly it was bright, for no Mexican buys electricity and shades it half away. And it seemed warm to the students, it was warmer than their homes. When they realized that teacher was freezing, they added a charcoal brazier to the heat furnished by the cookstove, and took care that it moved with her around the room. She wasn't much more comfortable, but she was very appreciative. In summer they sat, as the children do, before a wall of honeysuckle in the garden, learning English of the most practical variety: "Good morning ... My name is Juan Valdez ... I am an American ... Good-by, I am going home."

Those who were able to read reported on a little paper in which news and information had been reduced to rudiments:

"Airplanes from the United States fly all over the world. The passengers have meals and sleep on the planes."

"Soybeans are used by many farmers as a green manure. The crop is plowed under. This is the same as adding manure to the soil."

"Pink salmon has the same food value as the more expensive red salmon. Salmon juices should not be thrown away."

"George P. Lavatta, Shoshone Indian, has received the Annual Indian Achievement medal for his service to the Indian tribes of the Northwest."

Lessons of this sort were pleasant and hopeful and desultory. The avid students to whom teacher gave serious attention were those studying for citizenship examinations. They must know some English, and they must have an acquaintance with current affairs. They were also poring over a simple history of the United States, and conning a textbook on citizen training. They were putting their backs into the job.

The atmosphere was intimate, the students felt happy and at ease. When a ruling forbade the use of a domicile for instruction federally sponsored, desolation spread among these men and women. They did not want to follow the project when it was moved to the administration building of Alazán-Apache Courts. But "teacher" went with them; and, after all, the place is their own. The San Antonio Board of Education eventually took over the work begun by the WPA in the kitchen of a Mexican home. Everything is grander, and the class seems content. But a residue of seekers who feel the need of Pascual's special contribution to life and learning still go to the house in the garden.

Nocturnal efforts to improve the mamas and papas does not, of course, disturb the school for children. It moves, as does its master, at an even tempo. But Pascual, seeking to make good citizens of his little Mexican-Americans—influenced no doubt by propaganda for hemispheric solidarity—lays great emphasis on our customs, and the year has its high points. The highest of these seems to be, perhaps because it is the conception most foreign to him, the observance of Mother's Day. An ailing man, a company of little boys and girls, make an effort which to Americans seems Herculean. But Mexicans, even Mexican babies, take it in their stride.

This is what they do: starting at midnight and continuing until dawn, a band of children walks through the streets of this vast quarter singing "morning songs" at the doors of their mothers. Sometime after eleven o'clock on Saturday evening the youngsters are deposited by their families at the school. The little ones may or may not have been bedded and napped in preparation for the wide-awake hours ahead; probably not, for early to sleep is not a habit with them. In any event, the children arrive, even the youngest, alert, bright-eyed, and smiling. Among them as guests are Plutarco, Agapita, and Juan Bautista Méndez. By eleven-thirty the company is assembled: the kitchen is full, the porch is overflowing, and in the garden lads are waiting quietly, playing happily, together. But they are all set for an occasion. And an occasion there is going to be. Led by Pedro with his violin, shepherded by Pascual, these children from four to fourteen are setting out to walk under the stars, singing the night away.

At twelve o'clock they are off. Through the gate, out of the fragrant garden, they pass into the rutted Street of the Birth. They are trooping along to the home of the nearest mother, there to present neither photographs nor candy nor flowers. They have nothing that money buys, they bring the poetry of devotion. And their offering seems to them the fitting, the inevitable, expression of their love, for people of a Spanish tradition celebrate many happy occasions with *mañanitas*. Anyone may be startled out of sleep on his name day by the voices of family and friends, or by professional musicians whom they have engaged to greet him at dawn. A guest may be awakened, a weary parish priest; the saints themselves are thus honored. So Pascual's conception is all that is most natural.

Pedro is leading the way through dim, uneven streets, past small houses that now in May are deep in flowers. At a certain gate he halts, raises his violin, and the children sing:

> Awake, oh mother dearest,
> Awake for it's past dawn,
> For mockingbirds are singing,
> And the moon has been withdrawn.

The Silver Cradle

The voices are thin and sweet. A door opens and a woman appears on the threshold. A child to whom this place is home advances, kisses his mother and murmurs some message in her ear. Then his comrades take up again the singing:

> Praise God! my stalwart brothers,
> A matin let us sing,
> For all of earth's good mothers,
> A bright good morning bring.

This being the home of a very little fellow, he stays behind and is consigned to pallet or bed as the others move away. But older, even slightly older, boys and girls continue into the night. Through the sleeping town they go, from house to house, from one rough street to another. At dawn they still are singing. And there is no waning of enthusiasm, rather does it grow. The songs at the last door, which happens to be that of the Méndez, are more numerous, the voices ring out more freely, than at any other:

> And listen, dearest mother,
> That in this humble lay,
> That in this fragrant morning,
> I wish thee pleasant day.

Felicidad, her long, black hair spread over her shoulders, comes smiling to receive the embraces of her children. Then, honor having been paid to mothers in the way most lovely that they know, Pascual and his charges troop off to early Mass.

They have achieved a miracle, these simple folk; they have lifted a conception inherently sentimental into the realm of beauty.

CHAPTER SEVEN

Honor to the Cura Hidalgo

Halfway through September the Méndez family, along with their compatriots throughout the world, celebrate Mexican Independence Day. Here in San Antonio the consulate is active, the Charros are busy with their colorful affairs; societies, schools, and individuals are expressing themselves after their own fashions.

But all the organizations, and the people at large, whatever they may be doing and wherever they may be doing it, are memorializing that September night of 1810 when Don Miguel Hidalgo y Costilla, priest in the village of Dolores, proclaimed that the time was at hand for Mexico to be free from Spain when he raised the *grito* that became the battle cry of revolution:

> Viva la Virgen de Gaudalupe,
> Viva la Independencia,
> Muera el mal gobierno!

The heads of Hidalgo, Allende, Aldama, and Jiménez had rotted on the Alhóndiga at Guanajuato; Morelos had been degraded by the Church and shot by the Civil Government; the land was red with blood and wet with tears before the proud Spanish regiments were conquered and freedom finally achieved.

It was, however, with the *grito* of 1810 that revolution was born. That is the cry raised by the president of Mexico, standing beside the bell of Dolores on the balcony of the great red national palace at eleven o'clock on the evening of September fifteenth every year. It is the cry answered with *vivas* and joyful noises by the people seething in the vast Zócalo below. It is repeated by schoolmasters and mayors, by consuls and ministers and ambassadors, by whatever symbol of authority prevails wherever Mexicans are gathered. While the multitude in Mexico City is shifting and shouting and singing in anticipation of the great moment, Latin-Americans in San Antonio are repairing to La Villita, to the Municipal Auditorium, to San Pedro Springs, to parks called Comanche and Cassiano, to participate in fiestas created for their particular pleasure. The Méndez family make their way on foot through streets that are either muddy or dusty to the Parque Cassiano, thus saving dimes for the treat of the evening.

Honor to the Cura Hidalgo

That unpretentious recreation ground on the western edge of town has become the scene of a *carnaval y gran romería*. Tree-shadowed and not too well lighted, with a sweet wet wind blowing in from the coast, it has the sense of a country fair. Between booths heavily decorated with greenery, hung with serapes and with Mexican and United States flags, the crowd is unhurriedly moving. Men in white aprons, girls in bright dresses, are calling tamales, hamburgers, wieners, and coffee. From a small table a family is offering rose or yellow syrup on crushed ice at a nickel a glass. Down near the pavilion a hatchet-faced American is doing a fine business in pink cotton candy. There are no tubs of sour-smelling pulque here, but bottled drinks of twenty names and one flavor are to be had. And in an arbor somewhat apart men are drinking warm beer.

The mechanized aspect of the carnival is largely in the hands of frizzled and weathered Nordics whose business it is throughout the year. They operate for charmed youngsters small merry-go-rounds on which blue and red and yellow airplanes have taken the place of the little carriages, the horses, and zebras of other days. To smiling old women they sell tickets for the Ferris wheel. But the more interesting of the games of chance are the affair of Mexicans: dark men with a faintly Arabic cast of countenance entice a public readily enticeable to stake its luck on any one of a dozen wheels, to have a try at marksmanship, to indulge in a game for which the basic equipment is a washboard and a handful of dice. The rewards for such ventures are peeping chicks and silent lambs, pottery and kitchen ware and heavy glass, carved sticks and painted sticks from Mexico, plaster reliefs of Our Lady of the Lakes made by compatriots of a nearby village, and full rounded figures of the Medicean Venus from heaven knows what place and hand.

Just outside the radius of activity is a sweetly simple picture characteristic of Mexican gatherings everywhere, groups disposing themselves on the earth and achieving in this public place, for a time that is of necessity brief, an effect of intimate domesticity: a very old woman with a child asleep on her shawl, a lad giving the bottle to his baby sister, families eating and drinking and talking quietly. The Méndez sit on the grass, too, and when a woman with a little boy comes by calling shyly, "Tamales, tamales," they buy some. This is a great treat.

Polycarpo and the older children drift over to the pavilion where a program is in progress. On a small stage, laureled and flagged, presided over by pictures of Hidalgo and the president of Mexico, the notables of the occasion are assembled. Any remaining space—and it is a good deal—is filled to the very roof by the more enterprising of the *hoi polloi*. A consul is at the microphone speaking of the glories of this sacred day. But since the people continue to walk around and to chatter without interruption, and the sounds of the carnival come in with only the hindrance of a chicken wire wall, the gift of oratory and the invention of science avail little. He is followed by three bored gentlemen from the city hall who successively do their duty as they see it. Speaking with commendable brevity, with complete unanimity of idea and almost of phrase, they wish the Mexicans, in English, "good luck in their war for independence," they hope everyone will have an enjoyable time at the celebration, they politely and relievedly say "thank you," and sit down. Then, just as some children are beginning a series of dances (which they perform, so far as one can judge by the tops of their heads, with verve and gaiety) the three politicians shake hands all 'round and take themselves off. The consul's party departs also for other functions in other places.

The pavilion is given over now to dancing, and music comes out into the night. People still are strolling and eating and drinking and succumbing to all the games of chance. The losers are accepting bad luck with good grace; the winners are displaying their coffeepots and casseroles, their figures of dogs and bulls, of goddesses and saints.

At the roll of a drum Polycarpo Méndez gathers up his family and leads them down the hill. A little apart and in shadow a dilapidated little circus is going into action. On a platform before a ragged, unsteady tent (but in the big top tradition for all that) stand three of the performers: a beautiful youth in a thin white shirt with sleeves delicately gathered at the wrist, a red sash tightly bound about his middle—a sinuous figure more elegant, perhaps, than acrobatic; a clown with face dramatically made up in reds and browns, a clown not at all in the wounding Watteau tradition, aiming at a more intense if less delicate interpretation of the tragic human way; beside him on that uncertain platform a double for the Duke of Windsor—a man with the weariness, the dissipation, and the charm of him who was briefly "of Great Britain, Ireland, and of the British Dominions beyond the Seas, King, Defender of the Faith, Emperor of India." Quite unselfconsciously he stands, a human figure tragic and engaging, waiting to allure the multitude: he is going to eat some fire. With a suggestion of effort, with a suppressed shudder, he does his stunt. The drum again, a little ballyhoo from the clown and the acrobat, then the Duke steps inside to take the money of such as are allured.

Polycarpo parts with hard saved dimes. And the enchanted Méndez file into a tent which has not only a ring but a small stage. An audience of perhaps forty people eventually assembles, but a good number of them appear to have been passed in. Certainly the acrobat with sleeves sheerer than those of any bishop comes over to sit by a sloe-eyed girl and to fondle in tenderly paternal fashion the baby in her arms. Certainly the little boy who climbs over seats and finally goes to sleep within the canvas wall of the ring has the air of being entirely at home. The clown sits chatting with his friends throughout the earlier numbers; and the Duke's companions, who are pretty numerous, address him as Panchito. Spanish is his tongue.

The tent with ragged canvas and slender poles, the unsteady seats, the stage laid with worn rugs and hung with faded green velvet monogrammed in gold—all these represent the penultimate in decent poverty. But over the poverty lies for some ineffable reason a patina of elegance. On one side of the green velvet stage are stacked, or thrown together, most of the properties the company possesses: a rapier, a swirl of orange velvet, scarred valises, a silk hat, and a heavy leather hatbox lined with crimson satin—an ancient aristocrat battered but unbroken.

Well, there is a violin solo, Charlie McCarthy with the clown taking the part of Bergen, the acrobat leaving his family to send a lithe body through hoops vicious with knives, a little dog doing tricks. That is all. And it is quite enough.

Then a woman with a ravaged face, in a sheath of worn black satin, comes on the stage. She recites with a sure sense of rhythm a patriotic poem. She is speaking, it is true, but she is also singing her beautiful language. Next the Duke, suddenly erect and serious, delivers an impassioned oration on the fatherland, its bloodstained past, its infinitely glorious future. The applause is warm and eager. Polycarpo and Felicidad sit with shining eyes. Even the children are pleased. It remains for a poor shabby circus to light emotion on Independence Day at Cassiano Park in San Antonio.

When the Méndez come out carnival is in full flower. Plutarco stops to talk with a friend who says softly, apropos of nothing at all, "At La Villita there is poetry and dancing."

He is quite right, there is dancing and the poetry of color and light and music. But that celebration is for people with dollars in their pockets. The Charro Association, which is dedicated to maintaining in Texas the rich costume and fine horsemanship of the great landowners of Mexico, has taken over the "Little Town." This is a group of old and middle-aged houses reclaimed from slum status by the National Youth Administration in co-operation with the city government, at the instance of Maury Maverick when he was mayor of San Antonio. It has been made into a center for arts and crafts, for Pan-American culture, and for international gaiety. There is a background of stone walls, of low delicate-colored

buildings, of retamas and Yuccas and other southwestern greenery. The Plaza Juárez, depressed a few feet
below the general level and with a stage at one end,
serves some agreeable purpose nearly every fine evening
throughout the year. Tonight it is decorated with small
pennants and with great stylized paper flowers. A loud-
speaker, alas! has been installed. Around the edges are
tables which will be used for convivial drinking and
visiting. Beer, soft drinks, and setups are available, and
hosts arrive unashamedly with their bottles. The little
houses are dimly lighted. From Bolívar Hall (the library
made possible by Carnegie funds) St. Francis of Assisi in
brocaded robes looks out. In a niche at the end of La Calle
de Guadalupe stands a small figure of the Virgin of the
Mexican people, and on a wall is an ancient cross bearing
the instruments of the Passion. Down La Calle de Hidalgo
there is promenading in a space too small for promenading. In La Plaza Juárez there is music, there is plaintive
singing, there is dancing in a space too crowded for dancing. At nine o'clock the floor is cleared. Into the plaza de-
files a line of men in the vast decorated sombreros, the
braided and embroidered and silver-buttoned regalia of
the Mexican *caballero*. Some of them are heavy and dark
and very Mexican; some of them are lithe and dark and
very Mexican. One has a face of carved wood, and the
essence of drama is in him.

The committee which is to choose the queen is announced, and young women representing various social
organizations and schools circle the place to be seen and to
be judged. Their gowns derive in some instances from
Paris, more often from Spain or from the peasant dress of

Mexico. It is interesting to note that these girls bent on gaiety carry about them a curious atmosphere of dignity —they may be stenographers today but maternity is their destination. As the *señoritas* complete the tour they take their places on either side of a high-backed chair which is the throne. One of their number is chosen and crowned—perhaps with a *charro* hat in lieu of a circlet of gold, perhaps by the mayor of the town. She is showered with compliments which are conceivably sincere, and with gifts which are certainly suspect of commercialism. Then the music begins and the dancing goes on. And on. Moving through the multitude, sitting at tables, dancing with their wives and sweethearts are the wide-hatted figures of glorified Mexican cowboys.

But Her Majesty has disappeared. She has slipped away to the official celebration in the Municipal Auditorium. There, since eight in the evening, a Gran Festival Literario-Musical (and perhaps athletic) has been in progress. The gathering, which numbers a few thousand, is being treated to oratory, to poetry, to music, to native dancing and singing; perhaps to the hair-raising performances of the Squadron of Death, a team of police motorcyclists which has come from Monterrey for the occasion; possibly to a choir of small boys from Mexico, the last word in good training, in infantile dignity and charm.

Just before eleven o'clock the newly crowned queen comes with an escort of Charros onto the stage. The red, white, and green flag of Mexico is delivered into her hands, and standing beside a young woman bearing the red, white, and blue, *Majesté régnante* becomes part of a patriotic tableau. The *grito de Dolores* is given by the highest official in these parts, the Consul-General of Mexico. All the world stands to sing the national anthems of the two republics. The great crimson curtain comes down.

Then the people are pouring out into the plaza. This musical-literary evening has been a charming occasion. It has been entirely free, but there have been many vacant seats. After all, it costs money and initiative to come from the outlying districts to the center of the town. It is certainly easier, and in many ways pleasanter, to express devotion to Father Hidalgo in some open space near one's own home. Truth to tell, he seems better remembered there.

The following day, September sixteenth, is full of events dedicated to patriotism and to pleasure. In mid-morning a small crowd is gathering before the statue of Hidalgo which stands on a green island in the swirling traffic of La Plaza Romana and La Plaza México. Delegations arrive bearing the standards of many societies— Hijos e Hijas de México, Cruz Blanca, Mutualista Monte de las Cruces, Cuauhtemoc, Sastres, Obreros de Ambos Sexos, and perhaps others. These organizations, most of which combine some form of insurance with loyalty to the fatherland, have come to pay homage to a village priest who had the good of poor people at heart.

Waiting in such shade as they can find are the *facultad* and small *alumnos* of the Centro Cultural Infantil Mexicano, together with their families and a few dozen well-wishers. Among the latter, rather surprisingly, are Doroteo Domínguez neatly brushed and wearing a white shirt, and Demetria Grimaldo surrounded by her younger children. Clearly visible across the way are the windows of Sears Roebuck, full of ready-made clothes and me-chanical devices. But the scene on the island is wholly foreign: a man with a tray of candy comes along, a toy vendor with wooden jumping jacks and animals devised of multicolored feathers; an ice cream cart appears, and youngsters run about with dripping cones. But not the *alumnos*. They are as grave as small judges.

El Centro Cultural Infantil seems to be in charge of the program. There is a declamation by a plump little boy in an open-necked white shirt and long white trous-ers, suggesting the Mexican businessman and patres-familias everywhere. There is an allocution by the Consul-General who is certainly a lawyer and perhaps a man of affairs, but who has all the marks of a weary scholar; there is a recitation by a child in a pink organdy dress and pink nylon gloves, as elegant in effect as ever her mother could make her. The directress of the school, who looks like the directress of a school, declaims a patriotic poem. The representatives of many of the societies which have come with standards and banners deliver discourses. Then various groups and individuals place their floral offerings. Some of these are large and costly, others are small bou-quets gathered in home gardens. The children of the Center of Infantile Culture sing the Mexican National Hymn,

Fellow countrymen, Mexico needs you
Have your bayonets ready to wield
Then ride forth where your fatherland leads you
Then ride forth where your fatherland leads you
To the roaring guns in the field.

[105]

There are the usual presentations and announcements, much greeting and shaking of hands. But the public is drifting away.

In the heat of the afternoon a parade moves through downtown streets: city officials in automobiles, some of them sparsely occupied; bands and pep squads, bugle corps and R.O.T.C. from various schools; men of the Sheriff's Posse sturdily mounted; the Charros, more picturesque than ever on spirited horses; their queen alone in her decorated car; representatives of many societies in automobiles gay with serapes and banners, but chiefly with the richly embroidered shawls, the wide-spreading skirts of the young women who grace them; the Consul-General in a car bearing the colors of his country.

This parade has as its objective the scene of the earlier ceremonies, the statue of the Venerable Cura Miguel Hidalgo y Costilla in La Plaza México. The Consul and his staff stand with the sun shining relentlessly in their faces. The Charros hold the salute while their queen places a wreath before the patriot priest. A burst of music, then slowly and solemnly the horsemen ride away. As the cars of all the clubs carrying all the colorful *señoritas* pass, one halts from time to time and a girl descends to leave flowers. When the last drum corps, the last pep squad, the last R.O.T.C. unit has marched by, the officials relax their stiff stance. With his own hands the Consul-General lays at the feet of Father Hidalgo the *ofrenda floral* of the Mexicans of San Antonio.

That night the Charros are honoring their young queen with a ball in La Plaza Juárez. At the Salón de la Unión the Hijos de México are staging a festival of "a genuinely national flavor," complete with music and dancing, with cockfights, and "all the games of chance the law allows." In the parks gaiety is repeating itself. Out on the rim of town the Duke is eating some fire, the clown is being heartbreakingly funny. In the darkness beyond the circus tent, fireflies are sparking.

CHAPTER EIGHT

Carnival of Memory

On All Souls' Day the Mexicans of San Antonio go to the cemeteries to visit with their dead.

They go in limousines carrying *prie-dieu* and tall chrysanthemums; they go in ramshackle carts and in ancient cars brimming with babies and blankets, baskets of food and garden flowers. Those who possess neither Lincolns nor Fords, nor anything in between, take the extra buses put on for the occasion. And those who haven't the fare trudge all the hard way on foot. For density, for diversity, for confusion on the road, only the circus crowd competes.

Carnival of Memory

There is an old burying ground and a new. To the latter more people go, take more decorations, create a vaster pageantry. Along the route leading to it bouquets are offered from the porches, the yards, the fences of poor homes; from tables and buckets and trucks by the roadside, even from the branches of trees! Near the gate, stands have sprung up, and florists have set out an immense display of plants and blossoms. At tables and booths families are serving tamales and tacos, hamburgers, cold drinks, and coffee. Boys are selling painted cans to be used as vases. Old men are circulating with trays of pralines and glazed pumpkin and sweet potato. Through the crowd the balloon man wanders with his opalescent bubbles.

For weeks the quarter has been preparing. Ten-cent stores have filled their windows with wreaths and sheaves and crosses of artificial flowers, together with black cats and witches and yellow harvest moons. A pottery shop has shown, among its pastel lamb and bird and boat *piñatas*, a black and orange witch. Florists' establishments, grocery stores, and mere holes in the wall have overflowed with arrangements of artificial flowers, often of great magnificence and cost.

In the last days of October outdoor merchants appear in the neighborhood of the market house. They bring masses of chrysanthemums white and yellow, lavender, bronze, and wine; crimson prince's-feathers; heavy-scented tuberoses; and the flower belonging peculiarly to this season, the yellow marigold. Ancient men dispose on the sidewalks such little red and yellow bunches as only Mexican old men make. Boys go through the streets pushing carts of frail wild asters, marigolds, and zinnias in barbaric colors.

On the eve of All Souls' a few bakeries may prepare special bread, usually in the form of a monk with a cross of sugar on his chest. And a handsomely produced annual with the macabre name of *La Calavera* appears on the newsstands. It is edited by the owner-cook of a restaurant called, of all things, The Shamrock Inn, and it is made profitable by the advertisers. On the cover is a death's-head and some such sobering phrase as,

> Memento, homo, qui
> Pulvis es, et in
> Pulverem Reverteris.

Here the solemn aspect of "The Skull" comes abruptly to an end. For this is a magazine of anonymous verse paying tribute to, or satirizing, figures so remote one from another as the president of Mexico and a midwife in Austin, Franklin D. Roosevelt and a local blacksmith. In between are lawyers, doctors, political figures, publishers, children of prominent citizens, and the director of Adina's Beauty Shop.

Of President Roosevelt an admirer wrote,

> "My Friends,"—is what he called us,
> Mattered not the color, race or creed,
> This man, the whole world loved,
> Whose courage filled our need;
>
> .   .   .   .
>
> Though he sleeps with the immortal dead—
> Still by his spirit, we are led

Carnival of Memory

His dream of peace, we must defend—
Roosevelt, our President—our friend.

A local belle was thus complimented:

> God took her from this earth
> And punished her in heaven
> For having slain a dozen
> With the beauty of her eyes.

A man who had best be nameless drew these lines:

> It may well be said
> Of this well-known skull,
> He died while drunk,
> Or from a frightful hangover.

Of another it was written:

> From his harem where he
> Played Sultan to a thousand hags
> Satan snatched him from us
> To place him behind bars
> And in a fierce volcanic fire.

To a small coterie this publication is of exciting interest, but the masses never see it. They are concerned with expressions more personal and more primitive.

All Saints' is dedicated to children who have "flown away to heaven"; but these folk are pragmatic, they go when best they can to decorate whatever graves they have. All Souls' is, of course, the day itself. Masses are celebrated in black-draped churches with a black-palled coffin at the chancel steps, and at the foot of a great bronze crucifix in both burying grounds. For this is a major holyday of the Catholic Church. It springs like everything else from the youth of the world. As Christian usage it is said to descend from the last Supper which was, of course, a funeral feast. In the early years of the era Mass was offered in the cemeteries and there was banqueting on the tombs—customs which survive to our own time. At the middle of the eleventh century, the Benedictines of Cluny designated November second as the day on which the faithful departed should be commemorated. The observance spread to other congregations, to other orders, beyond the confines of France, finally through the whole world.

Today, nine hundred years later, an altar is erected at the heart of the vast new graveyard in the western reaches of San Antonio. Hither comes the Archbishop vested in purple. Priests and altar boys and a choir of seminarians await him. And a few hundred people assemble in heat or cold or rain as the Mass for the dead moves on its stately way.

Others are passing by. All over the cemetery families are coming and going, ordering and making beautiful their graves. Down by the gate, in the section of the rich, are fine monuments and fine flowers, with here and there a marquee to create a little private sitting-room. It is furnished with a *prie-dieu*, chairs, perhaps a rug, and the floral pieces are magnificent. In one such shelter a young girl watches, quite alone. "We are five here," she says, "and each one has his little house." Beside the elaborately decorated grave of Ramón Hernández, "First Trail Driver and Wagon Freighter of the Southwest," his granddaughter and his great-grandchildren sit quietly. The plat of the Benedictine sisters is unadorned, as is that of the aged poor, R. McMonigal, benefactor. But the graves of the Belgian flower growers, a little farther on, are lush with finest blossoms.

Over beyond the Crucifix the crowd is greater, the decorations more colorful and even more numerous. To this area come the Méndez, variously encumbered. They unfold a chair for little grandmother, make a pallet for Refugio, and establish the two of them in the scant shade of a neighboring tree. Felicidad sends Juan Bautista for water. Then she sets about scrubbing the small gray headstones of her father, her elder sister, and her two young brothers. Polycarpo's dead lie far away, but he comes graciously to perform services of remembrance for his wife's family. He does a little weeding and tending, then he occupies himself with fastening white and pink and ruby, violet and flame and lemon colored roses on a tall cypress tree. The children are absorbedly arranging flowers in cans painted rose or gray. The old grandmother looks on with satisfaction. But she is not altogether at peace. She feels that they should have set out a funeral feast at home, and brought flower-decked platters to leave on the graves. Her daughter's generation in San Antonio has moved away from these world-wide and age-old practices, but it is everywhere evident that El Día de los Muertos remains for them a great and solemn occasion. When all is readied Polycarpo and Felicidad, with the aid and advice of their offspring, place on the graves wreaths and crosses of artificial flowers, bouquets from their garden, making four gay spots of color. The family gaze contentedly on their handiwork, they kneel while Felicidad says a prayer. Then spreading a blanket beside the *casas* of their dead, they open a *bolsa* and address themselves to food. They survey the scene with interest, they call to passing friends. All about them is activity and murmurous talk. But there is neither noise nor confusion. Rather is there quietude.

On a nearby lot two young men are working with passionate intensity at a grave marked *Madre*. They arrange and rearrange baskets and vases of fresh flowers, they add greenery here and take it away there. They step back to judge an effect, then they change this or that. Last of all they bring a great wreath of black foliage and gold roses and stand it on an easel beside their mother's resting place. Their lips move, they cross themselves, then slowly, backward-looking, they go away. A woman and two small boys are setting blue cans of yellow marigolds before the shaft erected in memory of Arcadia Álvarez, aged thirty, by her mother, her husband, and her sons. The little boys here today are apparently those sons.

On the broad base of a gray monument sit three black-shawled crones, the Fates themselves, for this brief moment without distaff and shears. A child in blue corduroy slacks has been set atop a tomb. Against another a woman leans smoking a cigarette. From a distance comes the sound of keening. Two girls seated flat on the earth are combing their long hair and reading the funnies. Before the piled-up earth of a waiting grave a family takes its ease, eating and drinking together. A woman in a faded cotton dress and worn shoes is placing costly chrysanthemums before a costly stone. A priest, with an altar boy holding a ragged umbrella over his bald head, wanders through these flowering acres. He is continually summoned, and the family kneels, often with candles in hand, as he offers prayers for the departed:

"Eternal rest grant unto them, O Lord, and let perpetual light shine upon them.

"Deliver me, O Lord, from everlasting death on that dread day when the heavens and earth shall be moved, and thou shalt come to judge the world by fire."

Now there may be rain on All Souls' as on any day, or a bitter wind may blow, but more often a hot sun beats down on acres of flowers: on wreaths green or black or silver, on roses gold or pink or blue, on crimson crosses and lavender crosses, on arrangements lemon, mauve or pink, on creations of every color. Somebody has left for Pantaleón Pérez a blue cross miraculously enclosed in a whiskey bottle. And somebody else has put red roses into the arms of a little Madonna made of concrete, somewhat in the Gothic mold. She looks five hundred years old, but she is only thirty. In many monuments photographs have been set. Over in the section where, as the custodian says, "all the *angelitos* are playing together," a small stone bears the pictures of three young children who perished all on the same day. A woman working nearby remembers that it was in a shack which went up in quick flames. A marble *capilla* perhaps two feet high was erected in memory of Roberto Jorge who winged his way to heaven at the age of three months.

It is recorded that this child of "sublime goodness and

unequalled beauty has slipped from the swaddling cloth of his lovely body," and that while "his parents are consumed with grief, he is living in eternal felicity."

The little edifice is vaguely international with a great star in the door, a cross on the spire, Indian-looking angels incised on the walls, and butterflies on the roof. The infant of virtue and beauty died twelve years ago. Today his chapel is settling into the earth, and the only flowers are three marigolds in a strange little wooden vase.

The grave of baby Romanita is a mosaic of lavender and white chrysanthemums, and on it are a doll's crib and seven little spoons. Another small resting place is outlined in blue bottles and blue light globes. A boy passes tossing cans into the air. A little girl is singing. Butterflies bestow a fleeting benediction.

With every hour the crowd is greater, the array of flowers vaster. Nuns all black and white, driven by a youthful member of their order, cruise through the cemetery in a smart station wagon. An old man and his apple-cheeked wife drive up in a cart jauntily drawn by a sleek donkey. Trucks, loaded to the fenders with people and flowers, taxis, cars from distant towns, limousines, and jalopies held together by wire and faith, follow each other endlessly along the driveways.

The light is fading. Now at last there is a sense of urgency. A voice is calling in English that the cemetery will be closed in fifteen minutes, another is crying in Spanish that it will be *cerrado* in eight minutes. People are streaming out, but people still are coming, still are unhurriedly decorating their graves. Gathering up their possessions and their obligations, the Méndez turn their faces homeward.

Birds sweep overhead, and birdmen, too. Cypress trees bend, black against the dying color in the sky. The scent of flowers is heavy on the air. Before the great crucifix a solitary woman kneels.

The gates are closing on this vast garden of remembrance.

CHAPTER NINE

Diversified Honors

At three o'clock on the morning of December twelfth parishioners of the church of Jesús y María rise blithely from their beds. They are going to greet with music and with song the dark patroness of their nation, Our Lady of Guadalupe. Throughout the little space of time that encompasses her feast day, the faithful manifest their devotion in manners most various: they go to Mass, present religious drama, march in procession, stage a cockfight, offer pagan dances, and sing *mañanitas* at dawn.

Before day breaks, windows are yellowing. Householders are coming out to light the little flower-embowered, treasure-strewn altars on porches, in gardens, even on sidewalks before poor homes. Figures are slipping through quiet streets, and before the dim church a patient company is massing. A band blares, voices rise on the night air:

> Awake, oh Holy Mother,
> For see that day has dawned
> And hear the Teponaztle
> That all the village awoke.
>
> . . . .
>
> Awake, oh Holy Mother,
> Awake for it is day,
> Imploring thy gracious blessing
> Find me kneeling at thy feet.

A sense of waiting. Then women, the Guadalupanas of the parish, are singing little morning songs to the Virgin. Musicians with violins and guitars and instruments unnamed appear, and before the closed door offer the plaintive melodies of their country. They depart, and others take their places. The crowd is growing, growing. Charros in swinging white capes or rich-colored serapes arrive with artists from Mexico. Then from every side there is music, there is song.

At half past four, bells peal. A pattern of electric light blazes on the stark façade. The doors open, and singing freely, the people pass within. The place is cold and shadowy, before the Virgin of Guadalupe a single light burns clearly. In the spandrels of the arches the red and white and green of Mexico is draped, and across the nave stretch ribbons of pink petals. High in the windows of the apse silver curtains incongruous gleam. All is quiet, but the pews are filling. Nobody is too old to come, and scarcely anybody is too young. Babies are brought with their bottles, and toddlers enter gravely. Pascual guides his small charges, Felicidad joins the Guadalupanas in the forward pews. Polycarpo leads little grandmother and the younger members of the family to their places. Jesús is there, removed, reverent; Doroteo, smooth-faced, reposed after long months in prison; boys in khaki, many young men sleek and dark and Latin. Now one section of the congregation, now another, is singing a *mañanita* to the

—most lovely Holy Virgin
Of Anahuac's fertile plain.

Then from the loft come the voices of the choir full and free. But there is no evidence of the clergy. This early morning hour belongs to simple folk and pious.

At five o'clock lights spring into life. Among the flowers on the altar candles flame. A space of stillness, of utter silence. Into the chancel comes a magenta figure, and kneels unmoving. A stringed orchestra, the voices of the choir, embroidering music of an ancient tradition. In a moment a flock of little boys in red and white, priests in white and gold, appear before the altar. The Church has taken over. Through the passing from side to side, the censer swinging, the intoning, that magenta figure is still as the saints in their places. Then it rises to a great height and preceded by an altar boy moves with processional dignity to the pulpit. A Mexican bishop has come to talk gently to an exalted congregation. Quietly he speaks, then powerfully. Again and again he addresses himself to "Madre Reina, protectora del pueblo Mexicano." In the rhythm of his phrases is always muted drama. Mass follows Mass in this church with its silver curtains, its pink streamers, its colors of the Mexican nation. About ten o'clock there comes into the patio a gay little procession, an old man and twenty children in varicolored costumes following the banner of Guadalupe. These are Damaso and his little matachinas arriving unannounced from nowhere to honor the Virgin of their fatherland. They kneel before her standard, and in the presence of a dozen chance spectators dance briefly. Then they go on their way. In the late afternoon Jesús Ramírez, the Indian dancer, comes to arrange with Anacleto some detail for the program of his Chichimecas next Sunday night. But Anacleto is occupied with the stringing of electric bulbs, the erecting of booths, the placing of tables, all the preparations for the *jamaica* which is set for the evening. Still, Jesús has come and seen. Tomorrow is full of time. He goes away content.

That night the big, bare yard behind the church is alive with loud music and harsh lights and poor people. Somehow they are making gaiety. Young girls in delicate gowns, chill perhaps in the December night, are vending sweet-smelling boutonnieres. Others in the costume of the China Poblana, a long, full-skirted, heavily embroidered dress, red, white, and green, are going about with trays of candy and cigarettes. Felicidad, in black with her mother's mantilla over her dark hair, shyly offers religious medals. Plutarco is selling cascarones, painted eggshells filled with confetti, which broken on a victim's head cause much merriment. Too many things are happening. Keeno players, among them a youthful padre and more than one white-haired great-grandmother, are staking their luck on figures of St. Anthony, Kewpie dolls, cans of peaches, and gayly colored sacks of flour—the last representing both food and clothing and explaining why little boys' shirts are sometimes one color in front and another behind. A group before the roulette table is intent on like rewards. On the steps of the school mothers are giving babies the breast. The Méndez children share with perfect equanimity an ice cream cone, lick and lick alike. Through the gently circulating crowd, youngsters skip and play.

Over beyond the bandstand, a greased pole has been set up, the most thoroughly greased pole possible to be conceived. And on the nearly inaccessible top of it have been placed spectacular rewards—five silver dollars and a twelve-pound ham. This is treasure beyond belief. Here men and boys are gathering, here gaiety is tempered with tension. It is with understandable emotion that a slender brown lad with a shock of black hair pulls off his shirt, folds it beside his shoes and, revealed in his skin and his oldest pants, approaches. Now, as we have noted, this pole is greased with the utmost liberality. Black-shock is pushed up as far as they can reach by eager friends. Then with passionate effort he ascends, or struggles to ascend, alone. Suddenly down he slides. Down to the very bottom. There is a sighing breath. Everybody from eager Plutarco to an enthralled young priest with his arm about Juan Bautista has been climbing with him. Black-shock makes the try again. He goes a foot, two feet higher. Then all this painful effort, all those dearly bought inches, come to nothing. Down he slides, down to the unyielding earth. That good pink ham, those five dear dollars, are as inaccessible as the stars. They are truly in the sky. He tries again. He works hard. He works harder. But each effort is more hopeless than the last, for he is always wearier and he is always greasier. Another foot, twelve painful inches, and he is sliding down. Gleaming with sweat, breathing heavily, he makes way.

For a moment the crowd is at rest. Now comes El Indio, an Indian of the Indians. Up he mounts in solemn silence, higher, ever higher. Higher than Black-shock. His face is not set, his body is not rigid; he is just climbing, gaining inches. He is at the halfway point. There is wild cheering. A foot beyond. Two feet. The crowd holds its collective breath. Then, in a split second, all is lost. The brown body is sliding down, it touches the unfriendly earth. Impassively the boy tries again. The effort is terrific. Up he goes. He cannot make his first high point. To the ground he slips. A wave of moaning passes through the crowd. "Sad but inevitable," it seems to say. El Indio utters not a sound, but he refuses to try again. He pulls on coat, thrusts feet into shoes and walks away. Another youth steps forward. Then another. It is always the same. Sweat and strain and struggle, and to no avail. When the fiesta draws at last to an end, the boys depart, longing. "Another day, another try," Father Nepo says. But the story of the five silver dollars and the twelve-pound ham had well be finished now. In the dead darkness of that night, notwithstanding the sacred precincts, notwithstanding the watchfulness of Anacleto, they were stolen. It could not have been by effort more determined. Spiked shoes must have done the deed.

While the eager youngsters are getting ready to essay the greased pole, the cocks are getting ready to fight. Or the semblance of cocks, for the church of Jesús y María is no breaker of Texas law. A small roped-off space, presided over by Don Vicente Flores, is the center of a good deal of activity. There are whispered conferences. Half a dozen people are getting ready to do something about something. Two little boys carrying huge bundles pass by. Then, suddenly, every one is quiet. Don Vicente assumes his most courtly manner, two cocks of a magnitude miraculous stand at respectful attention as into the pit steps the Virgin Mary. Graciously she announces that *The Four Apparitions of the Virgin of Guadalupe* is about to be presented in the auditorium of the school, and she invites everyone to be present at its pious beauties. Then, to a flutter of applause, Our Lady retires and the cocks take over. Now it must be understood that these magnificent combatants are none other than José and Juan, sons of Anacleto, their small bodies thrust into the fabricated skin and cloth feathers of a red rooster and a white. They are little boys, but they make great cocks. Released by *soltadores* who appear insignificant beside them, they go at each other with fire and fury. Spectators turn from side to side unable to make up their minds whether to watch this zestful combat or to face the intense effort on the pole. Amid delighted shrieks the cocks dash and gash. They attack with mirthful vengeance. The white is overcome. He lays him down with good grace, for he knows that he will live to fight another day.

The crowd turns to the greased pole, to the keeno table, or lounges about the bandstand. The Méndez go up to the auditorium to enjoy the entertainment to which they were invited by so exalted a personage a little while ago. The shabby, unpainted, badly worn hall is full of eager people who haven't many cents but have parted with twenty of them to see a talky little play which they have known all the days of their lives. It is, of course, the well-loved story of Juan Diego and the roses. The Virgin Mary, dark-faced and Indian, manifested herself to that pious peasant four separate times in the month of December, 1531. There is cloth and paint to prove it. Appearing at the foot of the hill of Tepeyac in the early morning of the ninth, she told him to go to the bishop saying she desired a church to be built on that very spot. This Juan did. His Excellency was kind but unimpressed. The Mother of God came to the weary and no doubt troubled man on his homeward way, and directed him to make a second appeal. Again the bishop listened to the good Indian, and this time he asked for proof of the story. Again the heavenly visitant was waiting for her messenger, and she directed him to come back on the following day. For reasons in themselves praiseworthy, he did not yield obedience to her command. But on December twelfth, bent on his own affairs and purposely taking an unaccustomed route, he encountered for the fourth time his persistent Lady. She told him to go to the top of the hill, and to gather roses he would find blossoming there. When he brought them to her, she touched the flowers and bade him take them to the bishop for a sign. Juan obeyed, carrying the roses in his *tilma*. And when he let fall his cloak in the prelate's study there was revealed, imprinted on the coarse cloth, a picture of the Virgin preserved even now in the great church they built at the foot of the hill of Tepeyac in accordance with her will. It is that high Lady whom all the pieties and all the gaieties of the season are designed to honor.

The play begins with the first apparition, a young girl in rose and blue, all silver-starred—a picture of authentic beauty. Then follow the successive appearances, interlarded with endless dialogue and a good deal of simple humor. The story is monotonous and the scenery is crude, but the costuming may be delightful and the young actors are wells of enthusiasm. Whatever its limitations, this is entertainment satisfactory to the people for whom it exists: *The Four Apparitions of the Virgin of Guadalupe* is presented year after year in Mexican communities on both sides of the Rio Grande. It is given in the auditoriums of various Catholic schools, occasionally by a group of amateurs as a midnight show at some theatre. Felicidad Méndez and her mother may see a picture produced under the direction of the Ministry of Education of Mexico which relates the story faithfully, but subordinates the miracle to the colorful aspects of rural life and makes much of pictorial effect. No matter. The spectators know well the legend. And they are quite equal to supplying the emotion. For today, indeed all these days, the spirit of the community is centered on the Indian Virgin who appeared to Juan Diego four hundred years ago.

Diversified Honors

As for the Méndez at the school of Jesús y María, when they come down into the cold darkening yard where the *jamaica* is folding up, where a little group stands anxiously regarding the ham atop the pole, where Anacleto is waiting to lock the gates, they are happy. They are like children, eternally charmed by an old story.

To Jesús Ramírez the mainsprings of life are piety and rhythm. By the mercy of God, one complements the other.

When he was a little boy out in the state of Jalisco his father, a Chichimec Indian, taught him the old dances of his people. And as a child of four he began to thud and weave and whirl with the men at those great religious festivals which for two or three days at a time take a whole community in their orgiastic grip. While his Indian father was teaching him pagan dances, his Creole mother was teaching him to say his prayers. Both lessons took hold. Jesús had, and has, the intensity of the artist. If he prayed at all, he would pray much. So when he was sixteen, he went to the great seminary at Zacatecas to study for the priesthood. There he worked at Latin and

Greek and many things besides. He had a passion for God, but it did not extend to conjugations. And eleven years is a long time to pad through conventual halls when what a man needs is to dance under the stars. Jesús stayed seven. Then he turned aside. He came to San Antonio. He married. He begat children. But discipline and education are not in vain, for he labors in the office of a produce company rather than in a ditch by the roadside. He has a good house with dependable roof and solid floors, he owns a radio and a case full of books. On summer evenings he lies barefoot on the grass reading dissertations on the social order. Under the guidance of Father Nepo, he is a leader among the men of the parish. Still, there persist in him those unanswered, urgent needs. Happily, they present no conflict: to express a religious compulsion, Jesús has only to return to the dances of his own land.

He does the obvious. He gathers about him old men and young men and slender reeds of boys—Los Mecas, short for Chichimecas, he calls them—and he teaches them the dances his father taught him. Throughout the day the men are occupied with the endless small labors of little people. Until darkness falls they have no leisure. It is fortunate that the yard of the church of Jesús y María, with open spaces, beaten earth, and strong lights is freely at their disposition. They dance sometimes on Holy Cross Day in May, always during the celebration honoring Our Lady of Guadalupe in December. Through the autumn they come on fixed nights to rehearse routines that by now many of them know well. But Jesús is forever taking a new arrow from his quiver, adding to the San Antonio repertory another of his twenty-five Indian dances.

Diversified Honors

Then, every year there are changes, some circumstance takes a man away, brings another to the scene. It is Jesús who is the center, who keeps the group a group. He finds aspirants to fill the vacant places. He interests a dancer who has come recently to these parts. He even takes on little boys and labors patiently with them. Who but the next generation is to keep burning this lamp of devotion? He sees to it that the costumes are right, fashioning with his own hands the tall feather headdresses, the wooden bows with arrows that click but never fly; sewing bands of tinkling bamboo around the short red and green and orange skirts; making sure that the *sonajas* (gourds) are variously and finely painted, that the mask of El Viejo and his chaps, jingling with four hundred *tonaletes,* are ready and waiting. The reward of endless care is that Los Mecas are a magnificent wild note in that mixture of piety and patriotism which is the procession of Guadalupe. But these chill evenings they are only tired men who have come in their working clothes to practice dances which came up from the earth of Mexico.

The feast of the Indian Virgin falls, as every one knows, on December twelfth, but in this parish of laborers who are free only before dawn or after dusk, the procession takes place on the nearest Sunday afternoon. About three o'clock there is a great commotion at the church of Jesús y María. The street is full of cars and people. The yard is full of small girls in the dress of the China Poblana, of little boys in the braided jacket, the tight trousers, and the wide hat of the *charro;* of tiny Otomies in the costume of the Mexican peasant, carrying on their backs reed cages holding toys or chicks or lovebirds, perhaps a

The Silver Cradle

snow white pigeon. Felicidad stands with the Guadalupanas, Agapita with the white-veiled Hijas de María. Pascual shepherds a "congregation" of small boys and girls. Jesús is waiting in the school with his barbaric Chichimecas. Anacleto is everywhere.

Presently there appears in the street before the church a procession that spans four centuries in the life of a nation. It begins with a car full of politicians and comes to a climax in an image of the Virgin of the Mexican people. In between are Boy Scouts and flags and banners. Tall cross and candles. Pascual leading solemn little children. Standard after standard painted and embroidered and gold fringed, followed by the Daughters of Mary, the Association of Christ the King, of the Holy Sacrament, of the Lord of the Agony. Boys and girls of a high school band. Long lines of Guadalupanas, little Otomies walking with their mothers. Gentle songs and prayers. Then another note. Julio playing his violin, Jesús with his Indians in feather headdresses three feet tall, rattling their gourds, clicking their arrows, thudding and weaving, bowing and kneeling, offering to a Christian saint their pagan best. Acolytes and clergy. A figure of Our Lady of Guadalupe carried on the shoulders of men. The faithful, singing. Then a float bearing the Virgin of the play, still rose and blue and silver starred, before her Juan Diego (aged four) roses spilling from his *tilma*.

With automobiles waiting at street corners, with trains rumbling and whistling a dozen blocks away, with airplanes sweeping low, before home altars adorned with flowers and pictures and trinkets, this procession of the centuries moves. Down streets sparsely lined with spec-

[130]

tators, back to the church it goes and the various orders pass within. All but those most pious Indian dancers. They make their steps outside. Then, ceremoniously, they retire.

While the priests and the people are at their devotions, Los Mecas, relieved of their headdresses, are smoking and jesting and enjoying the valued repose of men who have danced over a three mile route. That is something. But the light is dying, figures are streaming out from the church. Near the center of the yard, Anacleto is arranging on a table a picture of Nuestra Señora de Guadalupe. Los Mecas kneel briefly before her. Julio strikes up a tune, and the dance is on. Bodies are bending, tall headdresses are sweeping in long rhythms, brown men are breaking into those monotonous, thudding dances which are expressions of pagan vitality and pagan joy. El Viejo, in rigidly smiling mask and jingling chaps, carrying doll and whip, jokes and clowns and chases children; he drives back the encroaching throng, pushes the doll into a victim's face and raises shouts of laughter. To the slender strains of a violin, Los Mecas are moving through their solemn, savage ceremonial: *El Tecolote,* a thudding dance in which the owl, symbol of ill luck, is slain; *La Víbora,* an affair of sinuous serpentines; *El Indio,* a wild, wierd calling, a blood-drinking story of the kill; rarely, *La Trenza,* in which men of seventy and boys of ten plait the red and white and green streamers of their December pole. (This is no gift from Merrie England, the Indians were weaving the braid when Cortés came.)

As the night deepens, as the tourists depart, as even the Mexicans melt away, Los Indios dance increasingly for their own pleasure. Spirits rise, bodies are more rhythmic, the dancing is freer and freer. In the drawn faces of old men is a glowing intensity. Jesús moves with head uplifted, with parted lips and shining eyes, with a sense of exaltation. Today he is fulfilled. There is about the whole bright picture a certain solemnity. There is also passion— a violin in the night, dark, savage cries, the pounding of Indian feet. They would go on with mounting fervor, with response ever wilder, until they were wet and winded and utterly worn down. But here at the church they must submit to the limitations of institutional life: they may not dance the low moon out of the sky, they may not drum up the dawn. When Father says a function is finished, a function is finished. It is early in the night, it is not yet eleven o'clock, when Anacleto gives the signal. A last genuflection before Our Lady, and the season of the dance is ended for Los Chichimecas. They are wiping their streaming faces, they are rolling their cigarettes. Then, having delivered to Jesús their fine feathers, they are cranking their trucks, climbing into jalopies, coming back into the world of today. To Jesús, breathing heavily, pouring sweat, Polycarpo Méndez expresses pleasure in the dancing.

"When the mind and the soul are one," the weary man answers, "then all is well."

Polycarpo nods gravely. He understands.

Diversified Honors

On a vacant lot where the Méndez graze their goat, old Damaso is teaching some children dances which come down from their Spanish-Indian past. The most elaborate of these is the dance of the matachinas which, whatever its ultimate origin, whatever its variations in time and space, has for theme the Conquest. Damaso lives in a *jacal* with a brush arbor before it, set in the middle of a field seventeen miles down the Corpus Christi road. He works hard nearly all the year. With his sons and his sons' sons he plows the land, he sows the seed, he chops the rows, and he picks the white cotton. When the labor is accomplished his *patrones* (two Mexican ladies who live in San Antonio) not only are willing that he shall indulge his lifelong pleasure in the dance, they encourage him with gifts of green cambric for a tunic, broad ribbon for a decoration, and any small mirrors, odds and ends of lace and beads they have stowed away. So the old man comes into town to stay with his son Juan who has a small house and a large yard full of haystacks and woodpiles and chickens and dogs and, of course, children and flowers, not far from the Méndez home. Word spreads among his grandchildren, his great-grandchildren, his foster children, his great-nieces and nephews, among the offspring of neighbors (including Agapita and Juan Bautista Méndez), even of friends who live at some distance, that there will be dancing. The little boys and girls come running. For them fiesta is an inner need: combining happiness with piety, they are going to honor with their best pleasure La Virgen Morena of their people.

On autumn afternoons Damaso goes over to the grassy

The Silver Cradle

lot which is their practice place. Julio appears with his violin. And suddenly the place is full of children. They have come in the face of mild parental disapproval based on the argument that dancing wears out shoes. But the opposition is perfunctory, for twenty mothers hereabouts are busy with cambric and paper and tinsel and ribbons and beads, making out of poverty and skill costumes which are going to transform drab youngsters of the public schools into bright figures of an immemorial tradition.

Damaso, a youth, and two very little children take their places before an imaginary altar. Pilar and Santa head the *cuadrillas*, Julio makes music, and the dance is on. They call themselves matachinas, a term that passed from Araby to Spain. It means "the masked ones," and it carries in Mediterranean Europe the suggestion of a grotesque figure. But here the mask, if it exists at all, is vestigial, and the costumes are not grotesque, they are gayly charming. As to the dance itself, everybody will tell you—everybody from old Damaso squatting in his leafy arbor to a learned Jesuit in his varnished study—that it is ancient Indian ceremonial modified to Christian usage. Certainly the theme is the struggle of Spanish against Indian power. Various groups interpret variously that tremendous drama, but the routine always stems from the story of Malinche and Cortés. Let old Damaso speak: "There should be thirty or forty dancers, but sometimes there are fewer. The main ones are El Monarca, Cortés and Malinche, and El Viejo. When they begin the dance Cortés and El Viejo start fighting over Malinche. El Viejo is killed. They dance around him leav-

[134]

ing him their crowns and palms and gourds. Afterward they come back, dancing, to pick them up. While picking them up, they play him a tune. They lay Malinche down, too, and cover her with crowns and palms and gourds. Then they pick them up and dance some more."

Now that, briefly, is what they do. But they restate and extend and comment on the theme in ways strange to us and native to them. Damaso bears the simple title of El Capitán; the youth is El Monarca, the Emperor Moctezuma; a fat little boy is Hernán Cortés, Marquis of the Valley of Oaxaca and Military Captain-General of New Spain; a girl of five is his Indian mistress, that woman of capacity who betrayed to him her country; an older man or boy is El Viejo—her father, the Mexican people, comic relief, and a sort of marshal who keeps the crowd in order.

Before a background of chicken coops and tubs and flowers, with neighbors and goats for audience, the children weave their tragic story. Many of them know well this dance, others learn by doing. Pilar guides the small boy who is going to be Cortés. Santiago, who a few years ago was one of them and now is married with a child of his own, looks on for a time; then, he cannot help it, he joins in. Doroteo stops to watch, and in a little while he has overturned a tub, found two lengths of sugar cane, and is adding a drum to the music. Every afternoon is a little party.

Damaso has no such near relationship with the clergy as has Jesús. It is true that his *niños*, all fresh and fine, may appear at the church of Jesús y María on the feast of the Virgin of Guadalupe. But then, for them the gaiety is just beginning. They are going to dance until Candlemas at the homes of friends all 'round the town. Felicidad will surely bid them to the house under the great tree. Old Salvador, who for fifty years led a group of *pastores* players, may invite them to his *casa*. And Natividad, himself a dancer of ability, and poorer than poor, will offer a grand affair. Natividad is like that. But the scene that is of all the most poetic is at the home of Primitivo and María de los Ángeles out almost in the country.

The horse and the burro have been staked at a distance. The lamb has been tied under the shed, but he gets loose and comes to the party. The yard has been cleanly swept, as it is every day. Poinsettias are tall and red against gray walls, in pots innumerable winter roses blossom. Primitivo has stretched wires across the yard, fastened on them many little pennants, and in the trees he has hung oil lanterns. María de los Ángeles has covered a table with a finely hemstitched sheet, set thereon a picture of Our Lady of Guadalupe which has the quality of an advertisement calendar, and arranged before it candles and ferns and flowers. They place a few benches and what chairs they possess on either side of the hard-swept space, and all is ready for the dancing children.

It is early evening, the land is graying. There is the sound of a truck grinding to a halt, then the music of a violin, and down the rough, dimly lighted street comes the most charming little procession in the world: the standard of the Virgin of Guadalupe draped with the colors of Mexico; an old man in a green cambric tunic, decorated with a wide pink ribbon, wearing a headdress of tissue paper and tinsel and beads and mirrors from which pink streamers flutter; a lad similarly attired; a little Spanish boy, a little Indian girl; somewhere in the company a ragged gray clown; then twenty gayly dizened children in crowns and capes and aprons, carrying painted gourds and a sort of fan of paper or of feathers which represents, they say, a palm. They come with ordered dignity into the yard. They kneel before María's Virgin and, Julio playing a tune, the dance begins.

These poor folk gotten up in shoddy finery yet achieve a curious effect of ceremonial. By some miracle incongruities are not incongruous. Pilar, taller than the others, in a long, slim, pink dress with a lavender cape, crown of silver paper, and palm of crimson feathers, does not look like a Mexcian girl costumed for a play or ready for a party. She looks what she is, a figure in some ritualistic act. On the cloth of one child's cape is embroidered the Virgin of Guadalupe. Into the lace of another's is crocheted the Victor dog ("His master's voice"). Small Malinche wears a blue silk dress trimmed with silver Christmas stuff, on her head a silver crown; Cortés, an infant of four, is grandly gotten up in black satin trousers, ruffled shirt, and plumed hat. El Viejo is a figure for fun with a mask of goatskin and trousers of onion sacking, along the seams of which flattened beer caps jingle, and he carries some small, stuffed animal with which he makes great play. The symbolism is vague and various, but a boy in the audience believes that his clowning is an effort to divert the attention of the Spanish from Malinche.

Cortés and El Viejo, a small boy in black satin and an old man in rags and patches, engage in battle. It is, of course, the Spaniard who conquers; El Viejo, the Mexican people, who is slain. Now of the mighty river of history, these people know little, and that little not always well. They do see that the lively old fellow in whose antics they delight lies extended on the earth while the children dance around covering him with their crowns, their decorated gourds, their many-colored palms. He is, indeed, a festive mound. Later, when Malinche is covered, they say, "She is not dead, she is only resting. This is a symbol that there will be no more war."

Hour after hour these green and rose and lavender, yellow and blue and crimson figures move through dances that are monotonous, repetitive, and curiously alive—existing not as spectacle but as ceremonial. Damaso is released, Pilar has a sacerdotal dignity, small Malinche is a miracle of rhythm, but stout Cortés is only a little boy near exhaustion. At a sign from the captain, they stack their gay, bright crowns and palms and gourds. They rest. But rest means play. They run and skip, clamber over the woodpile, plague the clown, and feed the lamb. When Damaso lightly shakes his tambourine, they fall into line and María de los Ángeles comes with a tray of fruit and candy. They are delighted, even Damaso, even Pilar. They have not enough, these little people.

Then, at the call of the tambourine, the children come back to dance some more. They dance and dance until Malinche is drooping with fatigue, until the other little ones are stumbling. One by one they are gathered into the arms of waiting mamas. But the older boys and girls, Pilar and Santa and Luz and Agapita, Domingo, Juan Bautista, and Miguel, are dancing ever more wildly—it is an exultation of exhaustion—and old Damaso, at seventy-two, is footing it with the best of them.

The world, except for this pool of color and light, is darkening. The spectators are drifting away. The mood of the dancers becomes relaxed, fluid. Here and there in the yard a man, often an old man in patched clothes, rises up to join them. Suddenly Doroteo is in the group, dancing with abandon. They move into routines unrelated to the matachín story. They perform a ritual of the hunt, they "make steps" for rain, for the planting. This has ceased to be an affair of children offering their best to fair Mary of the Christians. It is an expression of the earth-urge and the God-urge of a people.

But all things, even a Mexican party, come sometime to an end. The yard is nearly empty. In soft light, the place seems sleeping. With utmost formality, Damaso thanks Primitivo and María de los Ángeles for their hospitality. He announces that next Sunday, in the afternoon, they will dance at the home of Polycarpo and Felicidad Méndez. Then, through the gate the procession passes. The dancers, in all their fantasy of color and costume, climb into the waiting truck and, weary but gently mirthful, roll through sleeping streets, home from their ceremonious, unpredictable children's party.

CHAPTER TEN

Royalty on the West Side

The chili queens have been banished from Haymarket Square. But no one thinks of cutting off their pretty heads, and like royalty more exalted, they keep a watchful eye on their former domain.

Driven undercover by the expansion of the market, the hostility of the authorities (to whom they were a headache on more counts than one), and the requirements of the Health Department, the Mexican families who operated the small, peripatetic restaurants known as chili stands have taken refuge where they could. Some of them have gone into hot cubicles along Produce Row where they dispense the same food to nearly the same clientele which frequented the tables that used to be set up every late afternoon in the open space west of the city market. They have decorated their "little cheap places" with bouquets of paper flowers and with pictures of the saints. They have purchased great white boxes to keep food pure, and they have installed facilities to supply perpetually boiling water. Their young daughters, the famous queens, are as always ready to serve and to charm. But the pungent odor of the cookery, so pleasant in the open air, is overpowering in those close-set rooms; and music is likely to come stridently from a machine, for the troubadours have stayed on the Square—all that is left of an institution as old as San Antonio.

When the first chili stand was established, no man can say, but the founder of a line of queens was surely a woman who slipped soundlessly through the grass to a place where Spanish soldiers were camped, and folding herself on her feet, with an earthen pot before her, waited for men to come for viands that smelled good and tasted better. It was a natural thing to do. And when the Presidio was built (that was in the 1720's), there must have been still groups against white walls, women quiet but expectant, offering to far-traveled, lonely men food and sweet companionship.

It was on the Plaza de Armas that the stands flourished for many a year. Hither people came for the functions of Spanish officials, for cockfighting and music and dancing; for the picture of dramatic figures 'round little fires, shadows playing on dark faces. But life was grim as well as gay. In those early days the narrow streets leading into

the square were closed at nightfall by curtains of tightly
stretched rawhide, impervious to Indian arrows, and
there is a legend that at the time of the cholera epidemic,
women deserted the stands to watch by the terrible deaths
of the dying. That was the apogee of the chili queens of
San Antonio. For decades they were a part of the busy
life of a market place, but when an Irish mayor built a
French City Hall in the heart of Spanish San Antonio, the
little restaurants were moved from Military Plaza. As late
as 1909, however, they were functioning over by the
Alamo. In that area they represented color and charm
rather than the fulfillment of a need; and they were pa-
tronized, especially on Sunday evenings, by the starchiest
of American society. Again opposition arose to undertakings so humble existing in a locale so exalted, and the
owners were ordered to take up their scant possessions
and trek westward.

They came to rest on Haymarket Square, and there
they stayed many a year. The space was occupied during a
twelve-hour day by a portion of the second largest outdoor market in the United States. It was crowded with
trucks from Oregon, from California, from Idaho and
Colorado and Florida and Louisiana, from the valley of
the Rio Grande, and from the fields of outlying San Antonio. There were masses of carrots and beets, of oranges
and grapefruits, baskets of silvery onions, heaps of purple
egg-plants, mountains of peppers red and green; there
were chrysanthemums and dahlias and yellow marigolds.

At three o'clock all this beauty and abundance departed. Then, when they were in favor, the chili stands
took over. Trucks rolled up crowded with mamas and

papas and babies, and the teen-aged daughters who were the famous queens; with trestles and boards and benches and chairs; with rudimentary stoves and piles of wood and baskets of dishes and cans of food. Skilled through much doing, the men quickly set up on either side of the plaza a row of restaurants, each consisting of long tables extending around three sides of a hollow square, the center of which was the kitchen of the establishment and the living room of the family. Papa and the older boys having done the heavy work and got a fire going usually departed—perhaps to larger leisure, perhaps to other fields of endeavor. Far down the line and in shadow were a few small tables lighted by torches, presided over by old women who had little to offer, and that little not good. They dozed often, and few patrons paused. The more enterprising families were at the end toward the market shed. There the mamas and the queens, whose number is limited only by parental fertility and the chance of sex determination, covered the tables with bright-colored, badly worn oilcloth, set out the necessities for eating and drinking, put coffee to boil, chili and tamales and frijoles to heat, arranged onions and lettuce and cheese in such wise that enchiladas and tacos could be made in a flash, and settled down to regard the world and to serve all comers until one in the morning.

They paid the city fifty cents an evening, and since they might take in twenty dollars, or thirty, they were engaged in a profitable venture. In cold weather, however, the patrons were few, and in case of heavy rain there was nothing to do but go home.

On fine nights they were a focus of unending activity.

The Silver Cradle

Behind the brightly laid tables families were receiving their friends, tending their babies, serving their clientele. The queens were murmuring together, calling their viands, instinctively wise in the ways of attracting the eyes of men, of repelling unwanted attention. Wood smoke drifted in the air, shot through with the beneficent odor of boiling coffee, the pungency of onion and garlic and chili concoctions. Cars drove up packed with incredible numbers of human creatures. Families like the Méndez savored such delicacies as they could afford. Workingmen stopped for a bowl of chili. Bums of the quarter, derelicts of human aspiration, lingered over a fifteen-cent supper. Furtive men drifted about, peddling perhaps the forbidden marihuana. Here, as nowhere else in Texas, Negroes sat down with Whites and never a word was said. Tourists came to dine gingerly, to relax in the atmosphere of a foreign land. The pitchman appeared with his tray of perfume and jewelry and trinkets. The leather merchant came along, hung with tooled belts and holsters, with wallets and many good-smelling wares. People issued from small crowded houses for air, for music, for the sake of mingling with their fellows. They moved ceaselessly, they talked in low tones. They were carrying on in the spirit of the generations.

While it was yet light, while there was still color in the western sky, the musicians arrived: an old man with an accordion, boys strumming guitars. Two children in the costume of the *charro* and the China Poblana sang brassily; with figures grouped about as dusk gathered they made a charming picture, but they were pleasanter to see than to hear. Later the minstrels were strolling in

the plaza, some in workaday clothes, some in the rich out-
fit of the Mexican cowboy on parade. Then, from here and
there and yonder came the music of strings; the voices,
now plaintive, now plangent, of men singing.

On an evening an old man, ill-fed, ill-dressed, ap-
proached the stand of María Vázquez and asked in Spanish, "How many tacos for a dime?" Then, shyly, "How
many tamales?" A queen answered kindly enough, but
her kindness went no farther. Too many old men need
food every night in Mexican San Antonio. As he was
about to turn away an American laborer told him to sit
down, and ordered tamales and coffee. The little old man,
his eyes bright, his thin face eager like a child's sat hesi-
tantly, tentatively, as though at any moment he might
float away. He drank to the last drop of *café con leche,* he
ate the last crumb of tamal. But he refused a second order.
Then, in Mexican-English he talked to the laborer, who
all the while was laying away food. Where did his benefactor live? Perhaps he could do some work for him
sometime. He took care of the yards of Americans, rich
people who paid him well, but in winter he was now and
then a little short of money. The host urged, rather
gruffly, another order, and the guest agreed, reluctantly,
to take away with him two tacos. While the tortillas
were being toasted and folded over a filling of chopped
meat and lettuce and tomatoes, in short while the tacos
were being prepared, the old fellow talked about his life
with his sisters. They had a *casita,* he said, in the yard of
an American family over near Alamo Plaza. It was a fine
place. The women did laundry and house cleaning. They
were busy nearly every day, and they kept strong. Him-

self, when he had missed a little time, he felt weak. But he was happy as he told all this. "It is a good life," he said.

And with his small, brittle bundle in his hand, he went away. Away from the dark vibrant queens, from this place of color and music and movement, back to the "good life" of poor Mexican people.

Now the royal families have passed from the scene. There remain on the plaza only the strolling musicians. They come at twilight with their guitars and their gourds to sing for what you give them. Ten cents a number is the expected sum, however, and a *conjunto* (consisting usually of two performers) may take in two or three dollars on an average evening. Since they may collect royalties on music they have composed, or add to their incomes by recording; since this is a good place to pick up an engagement to play for a dance, or to sing *mañanitas* at dawn; since, in any event, they are likely to have other work during the day, they regard an evening on the plaza as a profitable pleasure.

The sky is low, the buildings are in shadow, the universe is closing in. Soldiers pause to ask for well-worn favorites: "La Paloma," "La Estrellita," "Rancho Grande," "South of the Border." A car drives up loaded with young blades, and the troubadours make a concerted rush. Los Dos Manueles win out and, the guitar accompanying, they sing whatever the boys call for: "Cien Años," "Ladrona de Besos," "Que Dios te Bendiga."

Among the men who have sung on the plaza there are artists, their names little known in San Antonio, who make the records played in this and other lands. And those who have not died of some sad illness, nor perished on the field of honor, nor been stabbed in a cantina brawl, may be heard again on "Hay" Square.

CHAPTER ELEVEN

A Place of Frequent Emotions

When Felicidad Méndez has been safely delivered of a
child and is up and about again, she goes over to Ruiz
Street to give thanks to the Lord of the Miracles. With
the baby in the curve of her arm and Plutarco carrying a
bolsa of didies and bottles, she walks through the morning streets to His chapel in the yard of her friends the
Rodríguez. That charm has fallen to progress, that the
shrine is without beauty and in part badly built, is of no
moment to this heavy-burdened, happy woman. She
cares only that over the altar hangs El Señor, a stark,
black-bearded Spanish Christ, crowned with silver thorns,

pierced with silver nails, his skirt stuck thick with little silver arms and legs and heads and hearts (above all hearts) left by people full of faith and thanksgiving. She says a prayer, she lights a candle, she leaves a picture of the baby on the altar.

Then, taking the infant from the expert arms of Plutarco, Felicidad sits on a bench beside the house and watches the life of the place go by. Manuela Rodríguez de Rodríguez, part owner of this property and custodian of the shrine, pauses to visit briefly. But she must be on her way. Women are waiting at the door of the chapel for candles, and tourists who have come into the yard want to ask questions. Now Manuela might tell them that she belongs to the second, if not to the first, families of San Antonio: that she is descended from José Ximenes de Cisneros, who came with the Alarcón Expedition of 1718, and from a Francisco Xavier Rodríguez, of whom she appears to know nothing, although there may be much to be known; that her great-grandmother, Teodora Rodríguez de Ximenes, vowed this chapel to the Lord of the Miracles. But she says only that El Señor was entrusted to her family in 1813, that they have cherished him ever since.

Having disposed of the past, she comes to sit beside Felicidad and talk about affairs of today. The Rodríguez are troubled. This home and shrine belong to the seven heirs of Manuela's mother, Candelaria Ximenes de Rodríguez. How are they to divide a good house, an old chapel, and a religious figure that is not only revered but revenue producing? Felicidad cannot help them to an answer. She calls Plutarco from a ball game in the street, organizes the baby, and they start on the long trek home. Manuela is left with her thoughts. She may not know by what route the great crucifix came into the keeping of some ancestor of hers; she probably has no glimmer of what the year 1813 connotes in the history of San Antonio, but to that date she clings with unremitting faith.

It is thinkable that she is right.

Experts say that the figure is old, that it represents Mexican workmanship of the late eighteenth century. And proof exists (proof is a solemn word) that in 1802 an image known as El Señor de los Milagros was venerated in the villa of San Fernando. For in that year Teresa Sáenz de Zevallos, being ill and believing herself about to die, made a will in which she disposed of her earthly goods and looked out for her soul as well as she could. She desired that her burial should be with simple ceremonies and "double tolls of the passing bell," that her body should be clothed in the robe of St. Francis which had been given her by her son, and that it should be laid away without a casket.

She declared that she was married to Juan Romero; and although the relationship appears to have degenerated to the point of hostility, she bequeathed to him the marital bed intact, and she settled a debt he had incurred with "a thin sheet which was rightfully his property." She left to her daughters a bronze crucifix and a crucifix from Rome, a gold cross set with emeralds and five strings of genuine pearls, two metates, and "the little three-legged iron pot." But that which is pertinent to this inquiry is one certain bequest: "I declare that I promised to the Most Holy Mary of Sorrows and the Lord of the Miracles, both of whom are worshiped in this parish, fifteen pesos. I direct that this sum be divided equally between them, and that one Low Mass be celebrated, with one-half pound of wax candles burning before the image of Our Lord of the Miracles. Therefore, I leave my own coverlet to my granddaughter María Luisa in payment for sweeping the church during the entire nine days while nine Masses are celebrated. I direct that my instructions be observed."

She left "one blue shawl made of cotton to be sold for the purpose of paying part of the debt to the Virgin of Sorrows and the Lord of the Miracles," and a pair of fine cotton stockings for the same purpose.

She referred to the part of the house left to her by her mother, "that is the house which now belongs to the heirs of the late Francisco Rodríguez." She made "a free gift and donation *inter vivos*" of land inherited from her mother "which previously belonged to Francisco Xavier Rodríguez."

Then Teresa Sáenz de Zevallos, wife of Juan Romero, kin of Francisco Xavier Rodríguez, who bequeathed "a crucifix from Rome, a gold cross set with emeralds and five strings of genuine pearls," signed with a mark because she did not know how to write her name.

Was the Francisco Xavier Rodríguez referred to in this will the faraway progenitor of Manuela Rodríguez de Rodríguez who sat talking with Felicidad Méndez one fair morning? The matter does not seem to be susceptible of proof, and it is in any event of slight consequence. It would be pleasant to think, however, that the Christ to whom Teresa Sáenz de Zevallos was devoted passed

into the custody of her family, that he has given direction
to their lives through the years.

The common belief is that the image was taken from
the church of San Fernando (now the cathedral) because
of a fire. And the insistence of the Rodríguez focuses attention, for the moment at least, on the year 1813. That
was the time of agony in San Antonio; the time when
Spain and Mexico fought bloodily for domination in this
land; when men were murdered, women degraded, and
devastation was everywhere. The records of the missions,
kept at San José, were almost completely destroyed. If
there was no fire in the town, it was the only disaster that
passed the place by. For many reasons treasures of San
Fernando may have been placed in pious homes for safe-
keeping.

The conflagration which is a matter of history occurred, however, in 1828. The church was destroyed, but
it is known that valued objects were removed. A cousin of
Manuela's asserts that a young man called Juan Ximenes
assisted in rescuing El Señor de los Milagros. And thereby
hangs a tale. The Ximenes had been in possession of a
royal grant in the general area of the present chapel since
1765. On it they had constructed a great stockade, and
about 1819 they had built a *capilla* for the Indians. Family tradition holds that they were close friends with the
pastor in charge at San Fernando, the famous Refugio
de la Garza; that he ate and slept in their house for
months on end. It is reasonable to think that he was their
guest after the destruction of the church. Did the priest
then entrust the great crucifix to young Juan who had
helped to rescue it, whose family possessed a chapel in

which it could be placed? These are only questions. It is
recorded, however, that eleven years later, when Juan
Ximenes was an old man of twenty-nine, he married
sixteen-year-old Teodora de Jesús Rodríguez; that in
1852 they bought from Sam S. Smith, the first mayor of
San Antonio, "a lot of land on the west side of the Arroyo
San Pedro known as Lot No. 97, North Range"; that on
it they built the small, oblong room known as La Capilla
de los Milagros. On a remnant of that property their descendants live today.

Teodora grew into a strong-willed woman of marked
piety, and it is with her that El Señor has long been most
closely associated. Did he come into her hands through the
marriage with Juan Ximenes? That could be.

One of their granddaughters says that the figure was
injured by a fire at the church (when she does not know),
and that a devoted parishioner undertook its restoration.
While he was working on it in some little room, somewhere in the village, he was signally honored by heaven:
he received the stigmata. Overcome with joy, or with
awe, at the sight of Christ's wounds on his own unworthy
flesh, the good man died that night. The restoration was
completed without the aid of human hands. This was indeed a Christ of Miracles!

Another lady full of years and memories, whose great-
grandmother was one of "the women of the Alamo,"
tells a varying, but not a contradictory, story:

"There was a fire at the church and the image of El
Señor de los Milagros was saved by a man whose name I
do not know. He hurt his back in getting the crucifix
down, and the priest gave it into his care. But the figure

had been burned and the father wanted to restore it. He needed for this purpose a certain powder and the blood of a young lamb. Knowing that a family in the parish owned such an animal, the priest asked for it, but the little creature was beloved by the children, and the mother was unwilling to take him from them. Now there was standing in the corner of the house, or maybe in an angle of the gallery, an unloaded rifle. Just at that moment it fell down and went off. It killed the lamb! Then the woman said, 'Father, our dear lamb is dead, I give him to you.'

"The priest accepted, but maybe he was not too grateful. Anyhow, when he went into the room where they had set the image, he found a little bag of the powder that was needed. How it got there, he never knew, but he mixed it with the lamb's blood, and the Lord of the Miracles was restored."

Who was the man with the injured back? There are those who believe he was Juan Ximenes.

A third calamity occurred at San Fernando: in 1873 the dome fell. There is no mention of a fire, however, and the damage was quickly repaired. It is nevertheless worthy of note that Bishop Dubuis of the Diocese of Galveston (which at that time included this area) had served for many years as a parish priest in San Antonio. He must have known the Rodríguez and Ximenes families; and if occasion arose he may well have entrusted church property to those churchly people. In any event three members of the connection whose opinions are often contradictory have stated separately, if a trifle vaguely, that Bishop Dubuis gave El Señor to Teodora.

A Place of Frequent Emotions

Certainly it was in the early seventies that the present Chapel of the Miracles was built. Certainly Juan and Teodora were then well-established, even influential, citizens of the community. One of their granddaughters, whose father helped to build the shrine, says that the principal apartment of their home was a great dirt-floored room supported by cedar posts. In it the family lived and loved and danced and died. Presiding over all was the Lord of the Miracles. It was not fitting that he should be so familiarly among them, but they had no other place. Not yet.

The sons of the house grew tall and strong, and sometime in the sixties the elder, Wenseslado, went to war. Manuela will say in one breath that he was a soldier in the Confederate army (no record of his service has been found), and that he fought against the French in Mexico. An ancient among the kin asserts that he joined the band of Catarino Garza, which suggests that he served across the Rio Grande. Where he fought is of small moment. To this inquiry it is important only that Wenseslado, like Malbrough, went to war. And Doña Teodora, in an agony of helpless terror, vowed to El Señor a little house to be his very own should her boy come safely home again. She would beg the money—that was part of the promise.

Her fine, tall son did come safely home, and the mother was, of course, true to her word. Rheims itself could not have expressed her thanksgiving. With a little bowl she went into the streets—it was something of a sight, and something of a gesture, for friends helped her, and even family. Those who had neither silver nor gold gave posts and rock and clay; those who had nothing at all gave the strength of their backs and the work of their hands. But there is reason to believe that in the last analysis Juan and Teodora lifted the weight of the undertaking. And in the course of time, on the side of the property conveniently near to the street called Ruiz, they built a little room of posts set vertically into the earth and chinked with mud and rock. It was a Spanish room, and to it they carried the Lord of the Miracles.

Both the granddaughter and the great-granddaughter of Teodora married men unrelated to their family who were called Rodríguez. Thus it comes about that the place remains to this day in the hands not only of her descendants, but of bearers of her name.

Teodora and Juan, their children and grandchildren, their progeny to this day, are of the Catholic faith, and among them are deeply religious men and women. But somewhere along the line there has been a falling out with the Church. It is generally believed that when the priests wanted back again that which they had entrusted to some branch of this family, the custodians, or owners, refused to give up their wonder-working, money-producing Christ. Under Texas law possession over a certain period, provided the property in question has not been stolen, constitutes ownership. Clearly they could not be forced. The title of El Señor and the will of Teresa Sáenz de Zevallos suggest that in an earlier day his power was approved by ecclesiastical authority. And the impenetrable silence at the cathedral indicates that some importance still attaches to the figure or to the situation. "You will learn nothing there," people most Catholic will say. That

A Place of Frequent Emotions

at least is true. We know that the family has the crucifix and that the chapel is said by devoted Catholics to be on what they call the "black list" of the Church.

The *capilla* was for long the humblest of little dirt-floored rooms standing almost in the country. Flowers and ferns in buckets and pots and cans flourished beside it, multicolored laundry flapped on the line, dogs slept under the trees, and from the branches hung birds in cages. But the fame of El Señor grew with the years. People journeyed from far places. They brought offerings and yet more offerings of every sort and kind. Even in the time of Teodora *milagros* were left in such numbers that the family had them made into the silver thorns which crown the Christ, the silver spikes which nail him to his cross. The walls came to be covered, every inch and over-lapping, with photographs of brides and grooms, of ill folks and young babies; with drawings and crude paint-ings of people being saved by miraculous intervention from death by overturning automobile, by onrushing train, by goring bull and striking serpent, by electric chair and grievous illness; with finely written testi-monials; with small garments and wedding gloves and braids of hair; with a photograph of F. D. R. offered "in gratitude for the miracle of having him elected president, and with thanks to El Señor for so great a favor."

There have been moments of high drama here. A young man convicted of murder was doomed to the electric chair. Twelve hours before the dread moment his sentence was commuted to life imprisonment. And his mother ex-pressed gratitude inexpressible by going on her knees, be-tween eight o'clock in the evening and one in the morn-

[157]

ing, through the streets of San Antonio to give thanks to the Lord of the Miracles for his mericiful intervention. Now to walk on the knees from the door of a great church to the chancel steps is hard, it is very hard. To walk thus through two miles of asphalt streets is ordeal almost insupportable, but a concourse of people went with this sorrowing, thankful mother. One man held a torch to light the dark stretches. Friends spread quilts and blankets in her path, then they picked them up and spread them there again. She almost sank down on the way, and when she came at last to the chapel she fainted. But Rodríguez women were there to do what kindness could, and the grateful mother continued in a state of exhausted exaltation to the bleeding feet of the Saviour, there to satisfy her need. Suddenly the place was full of dark figures, kneeling.

The chapel is changed, very changed. It stands now between a busy thoroughfare and a great highway. Angelita Prado of Chicago has expressed thanksgiving for a son's recovery from a grave illness by adding a squat, square tower. Above it shines the date, 1813. The family has done first one thing and then another. Teodora's little room is plastered, the roof is barrel-vaulted, the floor is paved, the two small windows are arched, and the glass is blue. The *retablos* that not long ago covered the walls have been packed away with fourteen boxes and chests of their like in the attic of the house. But about all this plastering and paving and arching is the pleasant irregularity of work done by the hands of men. Over the yard, concrete covered, hot and hard, the washing waves languidly. Against the walls of the house are fastened bamboo bird cages without modern comfort. Something of the decorous order that informed the shrine in an earlier day is gone. Still, every late afternoon boys of eight or ten (Manuela's grandson and children of the neighborhood) are busily sweeping and dusting and ordering the little room. And they pause to make a pilgrim welcome.

For the spirit of the place is constant. Anything that has happened there since the house of El Señor was built, indeed since he came into the lives of these people, can happen there tomorrow. At the season of Christ's birth the altar is made into a vast *Nacimiento*, a sparkling landscape through which shepherds make their way to Bethlehem; and on Christmas Eve at midnight the matriarch of the family lays the Babe of Beauty in the waiting manger. On Good Friday the crucifix is swathed in a *chal* of finest lace, at Easter the place is massed with lilies. On a night of spring girls trail red pomegranate blossoms over white altar cloth; during the hot days of summer men leave flowers from the cotton plants, and later they come with full-weighted bolls, gourds, and ears of yellow corn. All through the year candles burn and people pray.

The chapel is never more its own self, never more appealing, than on some clear Sunday morning when the altar is sweet with jasmine and roses, when points of candles gleam, and still figures kneel at prayer. Manuela weaves back and forth with vases and water and candles great or small. A soldier brings a rude cross in gratitude for some mercy granted. A country-looking boy and girl enter shyly to lay a wedding bouquet on the altar. Polycarpo assuages the current baby while Felicidad intercedes with God. An old man kneels with head upraised and arms outstretched, himself a cross.

This is, in the words of the Abbé Dubuis, "a place of frequent emotions."